tough
and tender
learning

DAVID NYBERG

Objection, evasion,
joyous distrust,
and love of irony
are signs of health;
everything absolute
belongs to pathology.

FRIEDRICH NIETZSCHE,
Beyond Good and Evil

I have so much to do
that I am going to bed.

SAVOYARD PROVERB

National Press Books 850 Hansen Way Palo Alto, California 94304

contents

part four   respecting persons in theory

part five   respecting persons in real life

preface

This book was written because some day I want to be a good teacher. The training I got in school did not convince me that I had become a teacher, at least not the kind of teacher I want to be. So, this book is about some of the important things that were left out of my formal training, some things that I have learned since then, and am learning still.

I hope that the several different voices and the apparent leaps between some of the chapters do not seem so undisciplined as to be irritating. I must admit that the book did not follow the outline I had prepared for it; it behaved rather like a child and turned out to have a character of its own that, in the end, I had to respect. I'm not disappointed, but I am surprised. Writing this book reminded me of something Alan Watts wrote about travel: "Real travel requires a maximum of unscheduled wandering, for there is no other way of discovering surprises and marvels, which, as I see it, is the only good reason for not staying home."

There is a first chapter, and a last chapter, but the way from one to the other is not linear. The book treats the same group of considerations over and over from a variety of approaches and in a variety of contexts. In that sense, the book is circular. I have tried to make the circle large enough to include at least a part of everyone concerned with learning.

Each of the chapters represents a different approach to combining the terms "human" and "humane" into one, especially in the ways that big people treat little people. The central consideration in this effort is the connection of thought and feeling. In *The Savage and Beautiful Country*, Alan McGlashan (1967) wrote:

> . . . .isolated thinking and isolated feeling are, in fact, classic forms of madness: they constitute the two dangerous, closed-in worlds of the schizophrenic and the manic-depressive. But to marry thinking and feeling is not merely to restore sanity to the operations of the human mind; it is also to open new and urgently needed dimensions in human consciousness.

The beauty of this marriage is that we don't have to go outside of ourselves to sense it, to understand it; though they may be hidden, the marriage partners are within us and all we have to do is celebrate their union, their *re*-union. As Hamlet told his friend, Horatio:

>   . . . bless'd are those
> Whose blood and judgment are so well co-mingled
> That they are not a pipe for fortune's finger
> To sound what stop she please.

There are many people lounging, fidgeting, laughing, frowning, and talking to each other in the pages that follow. Though you can't see them, I know they are there. Don De Lay, Al Baker, Helen Schrader, Lawrence Thomas, Joseph Luft, Hobart Thomas, Opal Jones, Kieran Egan, Brian Brown, and Buck Wales have been especially generous in helping me learn from them. Palmer Pinney has been a conscientious, good humored, excellent editor, and a wise friend. My family and my friends Jon Emerson, his wife Ann, and Patrick Thomas have given me more than I can ever tell.

for my son, Jonathan

o the mysteries
and heroism of
opening closed things

Mix a little mystery with everything, and the very mystery arouses veneration.

BALTASAR GRACIAN, *The Art of Worldly Wisdom*

"My lady," he said, "I am not a hero. It is a trade, no more, like weaving or brewing, and like them it has its own tricks and knacks and small arts. There are ways of perceiving witches, and of knowing poison streams; there are certain weak spots that all dragons have, and certain riddles that hooded strangers tend to set you. But the true secret of being a hero lies in knowing the order of things. The swineherd cannot already be wed to the princess when he embarks on his adventures, nor can the boy knock at the witch's door when she is away on vacation. The wicked uncle cannot be found out and foiled before he does something wicked. Things must happen when it is time for them to happen. Quests may not simply be abandoned; prophecies may not be left to rot like unpicked fruit; unicorns may go unrescued for a long time, but not forever. The happy ending cannot come in the middle of the story."

PETER S. BEAGLE, *The Last Unicorn*

1

Remember the myth of Pandora? She was and still is such a troublemaker. Zeus had her created to torment that perfidious fellow, Prometheus, who had stolen the irate god's fire. Pandora (from the Greek meaning "all gifts") bore a vase or box with her that Zeus had filled with terrible afflictions. She, being naturally curious as to the contents of her vessel, opened it. The afflictions escaped and spread all over the place, and the only thing left in the box was hope. Zeus had his revenge. We were tricked.

I think we were tricked in two ways. The first is obvious: we got the woes. The second is a bit more subtle. Ever since that bad start, we have shown a distinct reluctance to get into things that were apparently closed to observation or discussion. Ourselves included. And most of the ways "things are done." We even fear to examine our afflictions. As Zeus would have it, the afflictions are simply there and all we have is hope, benign and fearful. This is an awful condition: the world is absurdly ill and we are in it, dumbly hoping that either it weren't or we weren't.

> Eluding is the invariable game. The typical act of
> eluding, the fatal evasion . . . is hope. Hope of another
> life one must "deserve" or trickery of those who live
> not for life itself but for some great idea that will
> transcend it, refine it, give it meaning, and betray it.

That was Albert Camus (1955, p. 7). Notice how he has

changed our predicament? Zeus gave us hope and Camus says that hope is a fatal evasion, as useless as suicide. Camus advises us to scorn fate and to act in the face of the absurd. Good advice, though my call to heroism is somewhat more modest. We already have the afflictions and hoping by itself doesn't change a thing, so the idea as I see it is to open other boxes.

There are two notorious boxes that come to mind right away. One is the Quincy Box, which is a name school architects and school planners have given to the dimensions of the classrooms in the first fully graded American school, built in Quincy, Massachusetts: it is still determining the looks, functions, and character of schools in this country. The other is the Black Box, which is the name some psychologists have given to that part of us that somehow mediates between a stimulus and a response or between a sensory perception and an interpretation or between a sensory perception and a consequent extrasensory or asensory perception. In other words, it's what people actually do inside.

A third box is what people refer to when they say, "Don't get personal" or "My feelings have nothing to do with this; stick to the subject." I call this the Shadow Box. Some people think that only licensed medical or psychological persons should be privy to the contents of Shadow Boxes. These people are, of course, Shadow Boxers. They are the ones who have a suspicious view of their brothers and who believe that to be open among them is not only foolish but masochistic. The result is a boxed-in, self-protective person who is perceived by others as a predator, behind whose silent nervous gaze lies the mystery of his power. When will he pounce? Do not provoke him, fear him.

A Black Quincy Shadow Box is a typical American school-room, which has things going on inside that nobody under-stands and which is full of people who are afraid of each other but won't admit it.

What are the mysteries of this triply closed box and what skills and knowledge do we need to open it? I believe that there are no great mysteries and that only two things are needed: (1) some of what the poet John Keats called negative capability, and (2) a little knowledge of and experience in the hero trade.

negative capability

In a letter to a relative, Keats wrote that what makes a "man of achievement" is negative capability, which is shown "when a man is capable of being in uncertainties, mysteries, doubts, without any irritable reaching after fact and reason." I think that a hero needs other skills too, but negative capabil-ity is very helpful on a quest. It surely is a disposition which would leave a hero open to new thoughts, feelings, insights, expressions, and the joy of being unbusy *and* close to what is happening in the present. It gives mysteries time to disappear.

Michael Polanyi, a brilliant scientist-philosopher, makes a distinction between *subsidiary awareness* and *focal aware-ness* (1958, p. 55) and says that they are mutually exclusive. An example he gives is the pianist who shifts his attention from the music he is playing to the activities of his fingers while he is playing, becomes confused, and has to stop or clumsily bumble on. I've found the same thing when I start to pay attention to the swing of my arms while walking or running; it breaks the easy stride and feels awkward. Focal awareness can block ideas, too. Polanyi notes (1958, p. 57) that "All particulars become meaningless if we lose sight of the pattern which they jointly constitute." It is utterly arbitrary and meaningless, for instance, to focus on performing certain "moves" associated with "teaching" when the "students" are literally or figuratively asleep. Some philosophers of education puzzle over the problem: Can you say one has taught when nothing was learned or when something other than what was intended to be taught was learned (such as the fact that this teacher is an awful bore)? The problem with this problem is that teaching and learning are being considered separately; the pattern of associations between people, their context, and whatever the subject is are ignored. The particulars "teach" and "learn" have become meaningless in their isolation from the pattern which they mutually constitute.

In the first paragraph of *Mr. Sammler's Planet,* Saul Bellow (1969) provides an example of what it's like to miss the feeling of negative capability.

> You had to be a crank to insist on being right. Being right was largely a matter of explanation. Intellectual man had become an explaining creature. Fathers to children, wives to husbands, lecturers to listeners, experts to laymen, colleagues to colleagues, doctors to patients, man to his own soul, explained. The roots of this, the causes of the other, the source of events, the history, the structure, the reasons why. For the most part, in one ear out the other. The soul wanted what it wanted. It had its own natural knowledge. It sat unhappily on superstructures of explanation, poor bird, not knowing which way to fly.

Mr. Sammler was at this point "seventy-plus, and at leisure." It shouldn't take that long.

Negative capability means resisting the temptation to focus on things too narrowly or too soon; it is subsidiary awareness plus good timing. It may lead to new and beneficial kinds of focal awareness. Thomas Kuhn indicates this in *The Structure of Scientific Revolutions* (1964, p. 121):

> Paradigms are not corrigible by normal science at all. Instead . . . normal science ultimately leads only to the recognition of anomalies and to crises. And these are terminated, not by deliberation and interpretation, but by a relatively sudden and unstructured event like the gestalt switch.

One of the main theses of Kuhn's evolutionary view of science is the occurrence of anomalies which, when not explained away as freaks of data, eventually but suddenly provide whole new views of things, new paradigms or patterns for further exploration. Science, he proposes, does not develop by incremental accretions, but by anomalous jerks. "Cultivate negative capability and one day become a jerk yourself" – a hero might try that one next time someone gives him trouble about his funny ideas.

All this is not to say that we must give up the ways of doing good hard work that we have learned and practiced for so many years. Before we get down to that sort of determined persistence, though, we should get a clear notion of what it is that we are doing, why it is important, and what it means in terms of the pattern of our lives. Sancho Panza and Don Quixote were a good team. Each of us can be a good team all by himself if we can learn to respect our lyricism as well as our lucidity, if we can have the patience to hold off explaining things that we really can't explain yet. Take time for silence, for silence is full of things to talk about.

the hero trade

Faced with that complicated (but not ultimately mysterious) Black Quincy Shadow Box, the American schoolroom, we are tempted to sigh that only a hero or a fool would mess with it. A lot of us qualify at times for the second category, having demonstrated a small mastery of foolish arts, but we prefer not to exercise these arts in public. Very few of us see ourselves as heroes, though, and that's because we don't really understand what a hero is. A hero is someone who, in the opinion of others, has heroic qualities. These qualities, as Beagle suggests, amount to a few "tricks, knacks, and small arts," including "knowing the order of things." Heroes are people like you and me; sometimes they have to hide and they all want to be loved. Their principal reputation lies in helping people who feel bad to feel better. This is done by finding out what is making a person feel bad and bringing it to light— every hero knows that bad things thrive in the dark and wither in the light.

The hero's way to the Black Quincy Shadow Box may be blocked by witches, poison streams, dragons, and hooded strangers. Here are hints for the hero who has not yet reached the object of his quest.*

----

*My thanks here to Jon and Ann Emerson for sharing their inside information on some of these points.

Witches always expose themselves, so there is no need for the hero to form a witch hunt. They always recite the lore of their trade before they do anything or allow anyone else to do anything, for without the lore they feel lost. They smile a lot when you are least expecting it, and the smile does not make you feel good; it seems to imply that the witches know something you don't know. Witches wince when you wink at them, and they are very uncomfortable when you laugh. The easiest way to distinguish real witches from people who only look like witches is to ask children. They know.

Many schools have within them three streams: one flows quickly by, one is wide and looks like a pool, and one flows backward. They are all there because of industrial necessity, and therefore they may be dangerously polluted. There are two reliable signs of their poisonous quality. One is when you see children sitting in them but not having a good time — just sitting there. The other is when you see a witch who looks at home in them. Witches like poison streams. These streams may block your way; they will always make it difficult for you to work.

Dragons are large and mighty, but they generally are stronger on the right side than the left, as the right side is covered with "sliding scales" which are virtually people-proof. However, dragons seldom expose themselves to the left, and so a hero should know two other weaknesses that the big beasts often have. One is for large numbers, whether of people, square feet of floor space, or dollars. When used as a lure, large numbers will distract a dragon from what he is supposed to be doing. The other weakness is for flattery. If you use it when he least deserves it, you can flatter the fire out of him.

Hooded strangers are forever blocking passageways (they have to do *something,* after all) with silly questions and riddles. There are two ways to handle this situation. One is to refuse to answer the riddle until the stranger gives you a good reason why you should answer. Press him on this point far enough and he will unwittingly give you the answer, at which point simply say, "Okay, stranger," and give the answer back to him. He will be placated and you may pass. The other way is to ask a known witch for the answer, for witches are in cahoots with hooded strangers.

The most important art of the hero trade is knowing the order of things. Heroes don't do anything that other people don't do, they just have a better sense of timing. They know that some witches are princesses in disguise and that poison streams may dry up and that dragons and hooded strangers sometimes retire and sometimes turn as if by magic into more benign creatures. Heroes also know that sometimes these things do *not* happen. They wait when they need to. There is no such thing as a pushy hero.

No one is entirely without a sense of order, despite what chronic systematizers say about "chaos" as the only alternative to *their* ways. A major secret of being a hero is taking time to find out what the other person's sense of order is and then helping him move around in it to his own best advantage. This is done primarily by getting the person to say clearly what he's doing, for if he can understand it well enough to say it clearly, he will know where he is and how to get to where he wants to go, or at least how to ask directions. This means a hero must be a good listener and a reasonably good conversationalist.

One kind of order grows out of living; another kind smothers living. Peter Marin (1969, p. 68) gives an heroic example of this difference:

> I remember a talk I had with a college student.
> "You know what I love to do," he said, "I love to go
>   into the woods and run among the trees."
> "Very nice," I said.
> "But it worries me. We shouldn't do it."
> "Why not?" I asked.
> "Because we get excited. It isn't *orderly.*"
> "Not orderly?"
> "Not orderly."
> "Do you run into the trees?" I asked.
> "Of course not."
> "Then it's orderly," I said.

Marin then suggests that people in schools tend to mistake stillness and rigidity for order. In fact, living is not stillness and rigidity; death is. A hero knows that most people want to avoid the deathlike kind of order, so he never tries to impose it on them. He knows that that kind of order is, paradoxically, a "form of human chaos" (Leonard, 1968).

the hero inside the box

The most effective way to open the schoolroom is from the inside, and teachers make the best possible heroes, for they have already reached the object of the quest. Of course, classrooms are frequently held shut by schools, and schools are somtimes enclosed by school systems. Opening these larger boxes requires more kinds of heroes and more extended attention to the order of things.

We should be clear about the word "teacher" before we go on. I do not like the word; it carries an implication of separateness which interferes with helping people learn. I agree with Carl Rogers (1969, especially Chapter 4) that "Teaching . . . is a vastly over-rated function," except in those societies, such as the Australian aborigines, whose survival depends on unchange. This is because teaching as instructing or imparting or directing customarily presupposes a fixed body of something to be instructed, imparted, or directed (the curriculum), and the size of the body then forces a teacher to "cover the material" at the expense of everything else that happens along the way. This form of order is still and rigid, in contrast to the living we do in an extremely fast-moving culture, country, world, galaxy.

The very old curriculum→teacher→student stystem, which grew out of a context that supported it, does not fit any abiding human context or the particular context we live in now. The material that typically is covered in schools, including the particular skills and carefully defined outcomes that go along with the subject matter, is unsuited to humans in general or inhabitants of the current world in particular. The curriculum as it stands looks like the work of witches and hooded strangers, with the cooperation of dragons.

The current world is changing so rapidly that the "teacher" should work toward developing persons who are flexible and stable enough in themselves to survive with at least a semblance of sanity and good feeling. That would be heroic, particularly in view of the senseless power given to the traditional curriculum on all levels of schooling. Joseph J. Schwab remarks of colleges (1969, p. 246), "As far as students are allowed to see, the curriculum is not a subject of thought; it merely is. In many cases, thought about curriculum is not merely invisible; it barely occurs." If the "teacher" had a real say in developing the curriculum, then it might focus less on the memorization of items discovered and more on the process of discovering, on the relations of persons to discovery and to each other, and on changes in the world. In any case, the "teacher" would have a new importance and would deserve a new name.

I don't know what a better name would be. Hall Sprague likes "adult helper." Carl Rogers likes "facilitator of learning." I sort of like "synergist" or "lubricator" or "the-only-one-in-the-room-who-gets-paid-for-being-there." The words don't matter so much as what the person does.

the hero and good conversation

If you are in the triple box and if the notions above make any sense to you, one of the things to do is develop a willingness and ability to have frank conversations with colleagues and students about the merits of the curriculum as it stands (or teeters) in your school; about the relations that exist among you and what you would do to improve them; and about the *rights* people have to pursue their learning in the ways they feel are best suited to them. The conversations may take toughness to initiate, but they can reveal the order of things and help you to open the Black Quincy Shadow Box.

Good conversation in a school is not just a way to discover the order of things. It is part of the order of things, or should be. John Wilson has written a fine essay called "Two Types of Teaching" (in Archambault, 1965) in which he distinguishes between the type of teaching that "relates to subjects which are not essential to human beings as such," and the "teaching of those subjects which each human being needs to master." His thesis is that all human beings want to be happy; knowledge of chemistry or Greek is not essential for constructing happiness as a person, though these subjects might be useful for some things and enjoyable; whereas "the ability to talk, walk, make friends, live at peace with your neighbours and express yourself sexually might be regarded as essential tools," tools which are really skills for achieving happiness as a person. The first type of teaching, Wilson points out, may be done with books, television, and other media besides a person. And if a person does this type of teaching, one needn't like him nor be liked by him to get the information. The second type of teaching, however, *is* human beings in communication with each other, *is* the action of getting on with each other, *is* the achieving of good feelings together. He goes on to say:

> To be able to talk and understand is basic to almost all of these skills; and it is very difficult to teach. The obstacles are not so much that the student has not read enough, or does not command a wide vocabulary or a high I.Q. They are psychological. People are frightened to speak, prejudiced, bewitched, over-eager, fanatical, and so forth. The difficulties can only be overcome by practice in small groups, run by a competent instructor. Herein lies the real problem; adults are not much better at talking than students. The image of the professor or the teacher, as it exists in the minds of pupils, is not such as to encourage communi-

cation. Perhaps the ultimate reason why this type of teaching is not popular is that we, the teachers, are frightened of doing it. For it is difficult and painful.

This reminds me of a remark A. S. Neill made about the aims of his school (Summerhill); he said he would rather produce a happy street sweeper than a neurotic engineer. (I would add that it is also more desirable to produce a happy engineer than a neurotic street sweeper.) In other words, it is more important, infinitely more important, how a person feels about himself than what particular things he can do to make money or fulfill someone else's social expectations.

I foresee the objection that "if that's all schools are supposed to do, morality will decline, the country will fall apart, and utter chaos will result." In the first place, that's not *all* that schools can do, it's just the first and most important thing they can do. In the second place, how can an increased percentage of happy, self-confident people who value themselves more than wealth or status be construed as a threat to morality and social order? In this objection, which I have heard breathed by several prominent dragons in broad daylight, there is the assumption that happy, self-confident, independent people will *choose* chaos! I think only dragons who are terribly frightened and guilty inside would believe that. Further, the action that dragon-people take to avoid such "chaos" is to increase their own power to control or eliminate the self-confidence and independence they fear, and *that* is immoral. It denies the competence of other humans. It prevents the conversation that discloses humanity. It keeps the box shut.

The possibilities for good conversation can be increased by changing the entire arrangement of schoolrooms – by opening the Quincy Box and replacing it with a setting where conversation is more likely to flourish. An effective change of this kind requires many heroes who work together. Even in a Quincy Box, one teacher may be able to exercise considerable inventiveness and encourage real communication through changes within the place. But the concern of this book is with opening the people who inhabit schoolrooms, and that involves the Black Box and the Shadow Box together.

There is no method that will guarantee communication, but there is a way to practice that strikes me as useful and hopeful. I agree with Max Birnbaum of the Boston University Human Relations Laboratory, who suggests (1969) that what he calls "human relations training" holds great potential for "improving education by dealing with its affective components, reducing the unnecessary friction between generations, and *creating a revolution in instruction by helping teachers to learn how to use the classroom group for learning purposes*" (my emphasis). Although his language is a bit jargony for me, I agree with the idea. He is talking about the same thing John Wilson and Carl Rogers (and many, many others) are talking about.

The basic idea is for "teachers," "facilitators," or whatever, to be in their Quincy Boxes and to deal with Black Boxes and Shadow Boxes in heroic fashion. Human relations training or sensitivity training or communications training or laboratory training or interactions training or T-group training, or experiential learning workshops or Gestalt workshops or transactional awareness workshops or encounter groups or growth groups (aren't these names tiresome?) or positive self-exploration groups or self-other confrontation groups, and on and on *ad nauseam* — all these have something to do with developing the willingness and ability to be in a classroom in a different way, for different reasons, and with different effects. Just what these group experiences have to do with being a teacher or facilitating learning is a question that calls for negative capability: the answer may arrive in time.

This book, I hope, will at least clarify some of the ideas that need consideration, and perhaps even provide some grounds for generating new ideas and ultimately new experiences.

vulnerability and sham

> Guildenstern: What is the dumbshow for?
> Player: Well, it's a device, really – it makes the action
> that follows more or less comprehensible; you under-
> stand, we are tied down to a language which makes
> up in obscurity what it lacks in style.
>
> TOM STOPPARD, *Rosencrantz and*
> *Guildenstern Are Dead*

2

When an animal knows he's vulnerable to danger, he tends to
protect himself. Man, clever creature that he is, has distinguished himself from other animals with his ability to *imag-*
ine a reason or need to defend himself; a clear and present
danger is no longer necessary to make him feel vulnerable
and in need of defensive protection.

Not surprisingly, Ingmar Bergman uses an example from
school to show this point in *Wild Strawberries:* an old profes-
sor, on the eve of being awarded his country's highest academic honor, has a dream of failing an examination. He has
still, after all his life, this terrible fear of being judged by
others – who doubtless dream as he does, the "Dream of
Failure" (Henry, 1963, p. 296).

This is not to say that paranoids don't have *real* enemies, too; it is rather to suggest that all of us have a touch of the relentless, imaginary fear that plagues so-called paranoids. Have you noticed a tendency toward stammering, sweating, or swallowing more than usual when caught in the act of revealing an honest feeling or opinion? If you have, it's probably because you're out of practice. It's relatively easy to be honest about those things that other people already know (once we have figured out what in fact they want to hear), but let's face it, we are not in the habit of being honest about those things which distinguish us from others or from the arbitrary norms (neighborhood or national) which bully us into denying personal judgments. We know that our differences, our deviations from the expected (more exactly, from that particular set of expectations we have allowed others to apply to us), are almost always real enough and intrinsically legitimate, but we are afraid of them anyhow. Once known by others, they might leave us open to judgment, comparison, and perhaps criticism. We defend ourselves from these imagined consequences of being open about the way we really feel by lying and deceiving. Sham.

Sometimes sham "arises from fear of retaliation . . . and because inner restraints interfere with frankness" (Henry, 1966a). An example of this might be the social studies teacher who is personally chagrined by the pap issued her in text form, who is especially mortified by the text treatment of slavery in the United States, and who is also quite aware that the men who pay the salaries have put the books in the room. The teacher, fearing trouble, presents the text *with enthusiasm* (having become familiar with theories about the teacher's responsibility to motivate students to learn even repulsive things), figuring the sooner over with, the better. That is sham: protecting oneself from criticism by people one probably doesn't respect in the first place at the expense of children whom one had better respect or get out of teaching. A smile, a pat, a hug, or an A for good work at this point does not make adequate recompense to the students. It serves to reinforce the deception.

It is ironic that most of us, who recognize part of ourselves in this example, at the same time claim honesty as part of our social image and ask others to trust us. But so many of us can and do perform this perfidious trick that we seldom are called on it. We have a conspiracy going. Small children who still take delight in themselves as themselves tend to embarrass us in this regard until we teach them the fundamentals of suspicion, competition, and acquisitive ambition. Then they tidy themselves up into tight little knots just as we have done. They stop trusting themselves and others.

But it's not that easy, quite. The rascals insist on their integrity; they seem to be capable of enduring for years our most painful dissuasions. Very few manage to resist forever, though, as you might notice by counting the adults you know who are genuinely self-confident, joyful, and curious, and whose integrity, undiminished by age or position, encourages you to trust them deeply.

natural authority

Children are indeed vulnerable to various physical and social hazards, and they rightly depend on the adults in their world for help and protection. I say "rightly" because adults have a natural authority in this respect through their superior size, experience, and capability. Children have no trouble accepting this natural authority. It is part of the experience, the continuum of experience, of any child in any society. Some of the abilities and limits of children without adults are suggested by Richard Hughes' *A High Wind in Jamaica* and William Golding's *Lord of the Flies*.

The idea of natural authority is central to George Dennison's extraordinary book *The Lives of Children* (1969), in which he describes his experience with the experimental First Street School in Manhattan. Though natural authority is the key to Dennison's experience, it is subtle still to most of us. Because children are vulnerable in certain respects, they defer willingly to the aid of adults *in certain respects*. But there is a difference between the child's *giving* credence to authority and the adult's *accepting* that credence. The giving feels good because it serves a practical purpose; it helps to get something that is needed. The accepting feels good because it serves an egotistical purpose; it helps to show that one is needed. The child outgrows the dependence faster than the adult outgrows the need to be depended on. That puts the adult ego in a vulnerable position and at the same time the child is becoming less vulnerable. From the point of view of control, the adult is losing it and the child is gaining it. At this point, if the adult is vulnerable to the threat of being unneeded, he is likely to extend what was a natural authority into an artificial one, a constant one, an authority that rests on circumstances that *might* occur. The adult anticipates and suspects what the child might do, and tries to control it through predicting it and taking action according to the prediction. The child, who is living in a world of unpredictability (which is therefore interesting), wants to try himself out against whatever he might get into.

This wanting is the best disposition toward learning there is, but it becomes a threat to the teacher. Such a threatened teacher is likely to perceive the child's reluctance to bow to imposed authority, whether needed or not, as a judgment of his personal qualifications as a teacher. If the teacher doesn't try to discover the reason for the child's reluctance, if indeed the situation does not require the teacher's intervention, the child is likely to become the butt of an even more irrational exercise in the defensive sally—he will be punished for having tried to express himself unpredictably, independent of authority. It's easy to see what that can lead to.

The trouble lies in the assumption that because an adult has a natural authority, he *is* an authority—or more accurately, the image of authority. What was a workable relation between the child and the adult becomes an abstraction spun about the adult like cotton candy; it's all in the appearance, for there is literally no substance to it. It is pitiful to hear this image's voice when it is challenged, because it is a sham voice, bluffing, rebuking, pleading, or archly indignant. And usually it is dedicated to silencing those other voices all around it which, rising out of individual solitudes, are trying to make the image go away. It's hard for the others to be friends with a sham because they have to be so careful.

learning sham

Adult sham comes as a blow to a child, and it creates an artificial and terrible sense of vulnerability because he has *be-*

lieved, seen his belief belied, and been told to believe still. A child believes in another person with an innocent sense of clarity about his relation with that person – trust. When this clarity is violated by an elusive, ethereal mirage, when the adult evokes his image and the child finds himself dealing with a level of status instead of the person who was there before, he is confused and perhaps frightened. The sham*or* is obviously trying to fortify a spurious sense of security in himself, but the effect on the sham*ee* is to deeply injure his sense of security and to make him feel more vulnerable to invisible things. There is a proverb to the effect that injury makes a man cunning. A child with an injured sense of trust and of security with an adult will become suspicious of trusting others and himself, his own judgment. Worst of all, he will likely take a lesson in how to be an adult; through his new experience in vulnerability he will learn how sham behavior can be a substitute for trust. He will learn sham.

The kind of sham illustrated in this case is the kind that derives from self-deception, "in the sense that we believe that by concealing the truth we are doing the other person good" (Henry, 1966a). And for this favor we expect thanks in the form of a willingness to believe and share in the sham. It is difficult to lie alone. A good lie, a lasting one, needs a lot of help to survive. Albee has written two dramatic examples of this in *Who's Afraid of Virginia Woolf* and *Tiny Alice.* In *Virginia Woolf* it's the sham son who finally is put to death; the image is given up by George as a last resort to regain the life he and his wife had sacrificed to an illusion. The complicity of sham in *Tiny Alice,* however, is shared by too many – all the characters but one – and in the end wins out: Julian, whose "weakness" is his inability to accept the sham, is shot in the stomach and left to bleed to death on an empty stage, for his own good, of course.

This notion of doing someone good by concealing truth, more by ambiguity than outright lying in most cases, is a peculiar one. For instance, we don't like to show death to children or even talk about it because we are afraid they will be frightened. We fail to realize that children perceive this avoidance, which acts to sustain the mystery behind it and also to imply that the adults themselves are afraid. Therefore the mysterious thing that even adults are afraid of *becomes* awfully frightening. We could say the same for what most children have to go through to learn about sex.

Once a child is initiated into the theater of vulnerability and sham, a serious actor's dilemma follows. The child finds that he can establish a repertoire of responses and rehearse them well only at the expense of his ability to will his own actions. The basic component of character strength, the ability to will effectively, diminishes as the social image, the acquired repertoire of responses, displaces the will. This diminished ability to will effectively in terms of his own unique personal style is overcome by a defensive will to seem. The will to seem is not common among animals other than man. The result of the practiced seemer is an uninteresting, ineffective, "successful," nice, bore of a person.

consequences of sham

The connection of seeming with mental health is documented daily, if not hourly, in the stories we are familiar with: "He always seemed like such a nice boy, so polite and well mannered; I just don't understand how he could do such a thing." The strain for self-assertion, for demonstrating somehow that one is really here and capable of producing some effect on something, for being a source of energy, cannot be capped and stemmed forever. And the longer it is denied the more likely its first expression will be violent (a form of frustration) and probably destructive (a form of hate). "If our experience is destroyed, our behavior will be destructive" (Laing, 1967, p. 12).

Our experience is destroyed when the attention we have for our own behavior and feelings is deflected from organic expression to artificial repression. Only through such a separation of attention from ourselves could we, for example, be *unaware* that we are yelling, frowning, or smiling as we are doing them. This phenomenon of deflected attention (Galt, 1933, *passim*) is at the bottom of much disagreement and misunderstanding.

The phenomenon has a bearing on how one feels about oneself, too. As Becker (1969, pp. 12-13) suggests, "self-esteem" is defined in the exercise of one's executive powers on objects, in one's active powers. It follows that passivity and "self-esteem" are at odds. Willing to seem appears to be a basically passive posture, and as such is a threat to "self-esteem." As one reacts to highly imaginary vulnerability with a sham suit of social images in order to be esteemed by others, one loses esteem for oneself. If this is the case, perhaps we have an explanation for the peculiar results we get from trying to follow the Old Testament teaching, "Love thy neighbor as thyself." We don't love ourselves very much, so we don't love our neighbors much, either. We do a lot of moralistic preaching instead.

We can be terribly jealous of people who are obviously,

seriously involved with themselves and their projects, jealous to the point of wanting to hamper or even hurt them. We want to be like them because they are doing what they really want to do, and they are not being shackled and made awkward by someone else's notion of what they should like or be like. They don't have to spend so much time patching leaks and cracks in an imaginary person trying to avoid the imaginary sources of fear which focus its life. We are jealous of them because we know (at certain terrible moments) that accepting the task of living in an image, a social image, carries the implication that images are somehow better, more acceptable, than ourselves, that we concrete persons are inferior to a contrived phantom, a shadow, a substanceless image.

Among vulnerable people fault is a big issue. Assigning it to someone else is a way of dissociating him from us, a way of evening things up. Blaming is often done freely and sometimes ruthlessly because it serves in a distorted way to counteract that overwhelming sense of powerless vulnerability we feel when we do not feel trust. Where there is no trust, there is always blame.

A person who offers a phantom to be perceived will achieve a phantom normalcy via a phantom acceptance (Goffman, 1963, p. 122). When a person feels vulnerable enough to create a phantom, an imitation of himself, he also creates a need to protect the imitation. To do this he must be alert to potential dangers, to approaching enemies of the phantom. One result of this sort of posturing is a change in perceptual focus—the need to *anticipate* draws attention to the periphery of a situation, where ambush is feared. This outer perceptual focus necessarily detracts from the center, the point of a particular situation or context. As the phantom scans for the threat which might surprise him, he loses touch with the close world around him, and the persons in this close world will get the feeling that "he isn't really here," or "he really doesn't care," or "we don't mean much to him." The close world will become a closed world.

Routing attention away from one's organic, expressive functioning to a socially defensive functioning leads to deflecting attention from those close to us to those we suspect as potential threats. It's more than ironic, its pathetic, that we can spend so much time and energy thinking about and trying to please or fend off those who are "after us" and whom we rarely respect, instead of spending that time and energy and concern with those who may love and need us.

sham as a consequence

Who is it that we try to please when we "fail" a child in something or other, when we use a grading curve, when we make up a lesson plan? Who is it that we serve when we keep the classroom and the whole school quiet, regular, and ever so tidy? Whose benefit and convenience are we thinking of when we separate by testing the "slow ones" from the "medium ones" from the "quick ones"?

In this sense, I think I understand what Thoreau meant when he said, "If I knew that a man were coming to my house with the express intention of doing me some good, I should run for my very life." Doing good for someone by asking him to believe a sham is asking him to be like us. If he acts as if he believes us, we say that's good and imply that he is good for doing so. If he resists the sham and calls us on it, we say that's bad and imply that he is bad (or disloyal, uppity, stubborn, impudent, irreverent, cheeky, troublesome, nonconformist, immature, odd, mean, inconsiderate). Whether he accepts or resists, we have acted in a way that expresses contempt for the whole concept of integrity.

"Good" and "bad" are terms that may have solid meaning, just as "authority" may be based on real needs, but quite often the terms are used as convenient labels for people and ideas we agree with or disagree with. It is rare when two persons who disagree are able to *agree* to disagree, without resorting to moralistic labels. When one or both of the persons speak from positions of sham authority, such labels seem inevitable.

William Galt (1933 p. 77) makes this observation:

> The fact is that the individual likes excuses, that he
> has become addicted to them. Everywhere his habitual
> set toward the social occasion is moralistic, resting
> constantly, as it does, on a praise-blame alternative of
> behavior.

The praise-blame alternative implies that upon disagreement someone is at fault: each thinks the other is. Also, we tend to praise those things we consider "good," which are things we like (in terms of behavior, what we ourselves do or want others to see us do) and blame those things we consider "bad," which are things we don't like (or don't do or don't want others to know we do). We teach children through our easy use of praise and blame that they are "good" when they please us and "bad" when they don't. How different it would be if children learned instead that disagreement was not blameworthy or bad, but something largely outside the moral sphere and more in need of clarification than of judgment. Instead, we habitually make judgments without clarity of understanding in our dealings with other people. We miss so much.

We want to feel community with others. With other adults, we go to great lengths to suppress differences and to fit norms so that we will be like the others and be liked by them. If our efforts fail, we have moral labels handy to explain the failure. With children, we strive to make them conform to us, and we use labels with more abandon.

And so it goes. The child comes to understand that if he doesn't please adults by being the way they are, by accepting the sham of their moralistic judgments (good = like me, bad = not like me), he is likely to suffer physical pain or humiliation. This suffering is caused by adults who tell him that they love him for what he is and that they want him to grow up with self-respect and strength of character. Not wishing to suffer that much and not recognizing that the adults are going through exactly the same pressures, the child gives in to the image imposed on him, a set of *ideas* about himself, a "good name," and begins to sacrifice himself for its maintenance – at least in the presence of those who would judge him.

That is sham nurtured by sham, out of which grows the extraordinary menagerie of imagined threats that make up the insidious vulnerability so many of us feel. We come to suspect every whim or feeling that percolates up, seeps through, or pops out naturally when we are relaxed or simply happy. Crippled weeping spirits with good names. Honor the child who doesn't fall for it. Thank the adult who doesn't try to make him.

feeling good
about yourself
and
creative noticing

A sweetness turned into a need, the need into a force,
the force into total tyranny.

HANNAH GREEN, *I Never Promised You A Rose Garden*

3

A good repair job is better than a bad invention, especially
when it's your own self you're concerned with. A person who
recovers his own strength is better off than the one who lives
on borrowed powers. Rube Goldberg's fantastical machines,
those super-complicated ways of doing the simplest things,
are like the tippy-toe arabesques we go through to avoid our
own ignorance, to avoid the simple admission, "I don't know,"
or "You're right; I'm wrong." To make such an admission requires a sense of integrity stronger than the sense of image
we try to cultivate. Integrity is integral strength; an image is

contrived from borrowed powers. Recognition of borrowed powers – the filigree we use to substitute for strength – and the experience of renouncing such powers are necessary for repairing one's integrity, one's integral strength. This idea is eloquently expressed in Eldridge Cleaver's first book, *Soul on Ice* (1968).

Integral strength and borrowed powers are related to the efforts all people make toward feeling good about themselves. The contemporary catchword for feeling good about yourself is self-esteem. Great volumes of research have been published to prove that on the whole most people prefer to feel good about themselves and that as a rule other people are rather ingenious about making it difficult or impossible to do so. The everyday example of this cultural cul-de-sac is the person who feels a weakness in some part of his character or competence, and instead of doing something about understanding and eliminating the weakness, he fortifies it by searching out weaknesses in other people which he can play on, thereby creating a comparison which is supposed to save his face. The accomplished apple licker will often talk about the apple behind his back; the liberal will stay locked in uncomfortable silence while sharing company with minority (if he's white) or majority (if not white) groups, though he will take pride in treating the other group's children just like his own group's children, and he will denounce the outspoken racists who live out of town.

If integral strength is a sign that you feel good about yourself, then borrowed powers (from other persons or from institutions) might be a sign of a deficiency in good feeling about yourself. This is not to say that it isn't splendid to share yourself with others; it's simply to suggest that borrowing is much less satisfying than sharing, and that nobody likes to borrow all the time anyway – much less lend. Borrowing gets you in debt.

Feeling good about yourself is necessary for doing most things well (with the likely exception of perfecting a personal style of masochism), and it is certainly necessary for sensing any joy in being conscious. It would therefore seem to me that all the motivation junk that teachers are supposed to learn and use on students means nothing more than learning how to notice what kids are telling you they need in order to feel good about themselves so they can get on with whatever mysteries are calling them. It should be clear that unless a teacher feels pretty good about himself, unless he has renounced as many of the powers he's borrowed as he can recognize, he will not be of much use in helping anyone else to feel good about himself. That would be like an old Tom Turkey strutting around the coops telling his brothers and sisters what a wonderful day Thanksgiving is.

There are some people who believe that it is not good for a person to feel too good about himself, in and of himself, for it is that kind of person who is likely to develop the audacity to excuse himself from the penance incumbent on him for having been born a unique human being. There are people who believe that this condition should be amended by demonstrating that one has become a reasonable facsimile of some other human being who is in turn a facsimile of yet another who was . . . This type of person will speak of the need for stringent self-denial, a sort of psychological prostration which is supposed to build character, and he will with great pride accuse the nonprostrate clans of being proud.

It is very difficult and not very interesting to be friends with a person who categorically condemns deviations from his own doctrine, who religiously confuses integral strength (integrity) with heretical egotism, and character with obedience. I don't want to talk about the fanatics who seem to thrive on this sort of master–slave relation, but I would like to talk about the ones of us who suspect that we are in such a situation and don't like it: those of us who have become flunkies — very small toadies indeed—in some slough or other, those whose curiosity has begun to atrophy and whose habits have begun to petrify, those many who experience a peculiar lack of pleasure or unpleasure in situations where *some* definite feeling would be expected. This anhedonic stupor is insidiously symptomatic of a person whose integral strength has been dissipated and displaced by borrowed powers from several sources (college degrees, organizational membership, family or community tradition, a boss, and the like) until there is almost no integral person left to feel with. His feelings are replaced with translations, interpretations, guesses, and analyses of whether some reaction is appropriate to the situation, of whether this or that appearance would be called for by this or that appearance. Feelings tend to muddle such calculations: such calculations tend to muddle feelings. Response out of feeling is not calculated.

If a teacher is trying to help a student feel better about himself so they can both get into some interesting work or project with some enthusiasm, it would be naive to merely manipulate the situation according to one or another theory of motivation without being clearly aware of the inadvertent teaching that is happening through the student's perception of the teacher's "silent language," his feeling, tone, posture, timing, and choice of words. In short, the way he comes across is obvious and just as influential as what he says. Ernest Hilgard made a strong point of this in relation to teaching (Hilgard, 1966), as have many others since (for example, Luft, 1970, Chap. 8). Maybe we could say that a teacher's principal effect is his affect.

If we are to distinguish between the malarkey of borrowed powers and the dignity of integral strength, then we must begin to notice how we go about noticing things and what others notice about us. In noticing we are also expressing what we care about, know, think we know, want to know, or don't know. Because this way of expression is so much taken for granted, it is rarely discussed and seldom understood as expression.

Our ability to notice involves two ideas which are antithetical and require each other (Whitehead, 1968, p. 4). These are the notion of importance and the notion of matter of fact.

We live in a midst. We are always in some context or other which includes things "brutely there," as Dewey once said, and a motion of relations which James described as a "blooming, buzzing confusion." We live in a constituency of existing things, of matter of fact things. Within this setting, though, we all develop a less inclusive, more personal context. It's our point of view, frame of reference, system of values, or some such thing. We develop it because we cannot see and respond to all things in the "matter of fact" world equally at all times. We make judgments of more or less, of this rather than that, to narrow down the field and gain some sense of place or control in it. Our judgments of more or less, this or that, are choices. Choices are expressions of value. Value in this sense is the same as importance; when something is important in our personal context it is of some value, and something we see as unimportant has less value until it becomes important.

Sometimes we get into habits of noticing, seeing the same things every day, or benumbing ourselves to what we look at but fail to see (as in looking at a clock and a moment later being unable to say what time it is). Habits tend to eliminate certain choices; when something is done habitually it is a repetition, without choice or change. I think we would all be completely out of our minds by now if habit were not available as one way of acting. Habits save a lot of time – I'd hate to have to think about typing while I'm typing. But habits can literally obliterate whole sections of the world, of time, of immediate experience, and for me that thought doesn't hold much comfort. Habits leave me handicapped in trying to develop a finer sense of importance. They bring an artificial rigidity which resists new interpretation, new connections, new meaning, new importance.

Importance can be considered an achievement, as when we find a new meaning in someone or something. Or it can be considered a permanent condition, as when some agent other than ourselves prescribes general rules for the development of human habits. In the latter case, importance becomes a matter of fact, mute and constant, much like a stone. The first sense of importance (as an achievement) has an element of currency in it, an involvement with context-in-process out of which meaning is constantly derived and checked. The second sense relies on principles independent of context-in-process, and it is static and rather imperious. This sort of extra-experiential importance, importance accepted as a matter of fact, is very like the borrowed power which substitutes for integral strength. It's the sort of thing that allows one to skip over or stomp on experiences with others by deferring attention from the experiences themselves to the abstracted source of borrowed powers. Galt (1933) talks of "deflected" attention as a symptom of cultural neurosis rooted in the notion of social image, which is an abstraction itself. When two people who are acting with borrowed powers, who have become social images of those powers, attempt to converse, they demonstrate what Abraham Kaplan terms a "duolog," which is much like the exchange between two television screens set face to face, presenting their respective programs to each other simultaneously.

Persons for whom importance is a matter of fact may be as hard on themselves as they are on others. Whitehead (1968, p. 21) notes: "The laws of nature are large average effects which reign impersonally. Whereas, there is nothing average about expression. It is essentially individual. In so far as an average dominates, expression fades." (This statement certainly touches the very personal aspects of some existential philosophies, especially and most forcefully in Nietzsche and Kierkegaard.) What is "average" is not precise nor exceptional nor intriguing in itself, but unfortunately for some it is compelling. Some people even *aspire* to being average! (Paul Goodman's notable book, *Growing Up Absurd* [1956], sadly enough, is still relevant to this point.) The world contains entire choruses of mumblers, inexpressive bearers of borrowed repetitions. It is impossible for them to achieve importance – to feel good about themselves as individuals with integral powers – so long as their adopted schemes of value prevent them from finding new meaning in new experience, that is, prevent them from learning.

Noticing is a powerful way to achieve importance. It is an expression of values and, like other expressions, it is affected by past choices and it serves as a basis for new ones. It is also a way to discover what is new and what is habitual in our behavior: we can notice ourselves noticing. To examine and to become more precisely aware of what we do in fact notice in different contexts is to reintroduce ourselves to our active valuations – to run a check on sneaky little habits and biases that may have infiltrated minds once noted for being open or broad.

Our habits and biases may be useful, and we may decide to keep them. By noticing them from time to time, though, we give them new personal valuation, and we guard against being petrified by them. Two kinds of rote noticing menace us. In one, we simply skip large areas that might be available to us. We ignore things in ourselves or others, sometimes for good reason, sometimes because we have become blind through habit and prejudice. The other kind of rote noticing is creative. Instead of skipping over possible new experience, we take the new experience and shrewdly find old meaning in it. This kind of noticing is found in paranoia and dogmatism. It takes ingenuity, and it resembles genius.

A genius is able to turn what he sees into an expression that adds meaning in a highly personal interpretive way to the object or situation perceived. This added meaning is basically a statement of perspective, open to be shared with others who are open to it. The perspective is often surprising. As practiced by a genius, creative noticing is an individual expression not hindered by the average or the habitual. In paranoia and dogmatism, though, creative noticing presents a high degree of predictability across circumstances.* That's what makes paranoia so painful and dogmatism so deplorable: the horror of incessance. Imagination is active in both cases, but regulated into a supportive instrument of fear: fear of being victimized in the paranoid's case, and fear of being unimportant and unworthy in the dogmatist's case. The meaning derived from new experiences becomes the same as that of a former, fixed experience. Documentation is amassed for an ancient conviction. What is important has already happened. New perceptions are transformed into old constructs and old meanings. This sort of creativity is antithetical to learning; it is repetitious in the extreme. It is also tedious, ridiculous, and very common in American institutions. It is almost traditional.

Ernest Becker (1969) suggests that a masochist is his own last center of attention. I think the same is true of the paranoid and the dogmatist. The first suggests this condition by imagining himself the object of others' interest; his work is to protect and preserve himself from that imagined interest which is also imagined as punitive – a projection of his own sense of weakness and vulnerability. His only recourse is to borrow shelter where he can, knowing well that it cannot be had. He is trapped by his interest in his own lack of integral strength: he is obsessed with his own vulnerability which is a manifestation of not feeling very good about himself – to put it lightly.

---

*"Creativity" is not always a positive force in a social or moral sense, though it is commonly thought to be. Hitler was, among other things, quite creative in managing his affairs. See also Kafka's story, *The Penal Colony.*

In much the same way a dogmatist gives his prime attention to some external power that he supposes will validate his existence and give him importance. He ingratiates himself wholly to the spirit-head or symbol of his belief, or he becomes a petty tyrant for the belief. Either way, he borrows power from a source external to himself. To assail his belief is to assail him; the belief is usually a system developed by others which he borrows and substitutes for the personal organization of his own experience. A confirmed dogmatist often becomes an instrument of the borrowed power, and he likely will act as if his inflexibility should be seen as strength of character. Inflexibility, however, is ultimately a form of servitude, a condition hostile to dignity and devastating to integrity.

A dogmatist wishes to be associated with a strength that he does not have himself in order to resemble a person of respect, a strength without which he feels impotent and meaningless. With his dogma he protects himself. He is recognized through his dogma, lost without it, lonely without it. In a sense dogmatism is like a catafalque, a scaffold on which the body of a deceased personage lies. The scaffold tends to restrict one's point of view, while making one highly visible.

Naming is allied to rote noticing of both kinds, negative and creative. On the one hand, we tend not to notice what we cannot name; on the other, if we do see a surprise we tend to try to make it familiar under a name or a system we already know. This basic perceptual bias blocks learning quite effectively. We cannot learn what we fail to notice, and when we do notice something we fool ourselves into thinking that naming it and placing it in a system amount to knowing it. Our engagement with the thing noticed is stopped as soon as the thing is brought under "control" through the repetition of familiar names in familiar systems. These systems of words and ideas are difficult to ignore. We are indefatigably drilled in them by our parents, teachers, and clergy. The patterns and logic of these notice-name schemes are dictated to us perhaps to ensure that we will see the same world that our elders think they see. In any case, the systems are so pervasive and handy that we tend to place any new experience in their context. We behave like mild paranoids or dogmatists, cleverly finding old meaning wherever we look.

I don't know if the menacing aspects of noticing can be summed up or not, but I'll have a go at it: To notice is to select, to ascribe significance in terms of security, status, or immediate needs. It is a functioning choice which is a valuing act. It is also an act of notation, for we seem to be uncomfortable if we cannot call a name for what we notice. The more desperate we are, the more vulnerable we feel, the greater the need to settle things down to get at least a semblance of control over them. This desperation sometimes takes the form of habitual blindness – of not noticing – and sometimes of paranoia or dogmatism, which may be seen as reducing all things noticed to evidence on a single theme.

Restricted noticing is both a cause and a result of repetitive behavior. Such behavior is shown in the ever-dying cycle of exclusion practiced by individuals, a redocumenting of the familiar which tends toward the average and the usual and which leads to stagnancy, stubbornness, and a bore of a disposition. The same repetitive behavior exists on a phylo-institutional level, where repetition is its own justification: that's the way it has been, that's the way it is, that's the way we like it, that's the way it's going to be.

Repetition is doing again what one (or someone else) has

already done, while learning is doing something else. Repetition is close in some ways to idolatry. There is nothing intrinsically wrong with the use of idols, symbols, myths, and the like—in fact, life is the more fascinating for them—but idolatry is dangerous to learning when the idol becomes confused with what it is meant to represent (Watts, 1966, p. 141). It's the old story of conjuring up an image and then taking it for granted and finally serving it as if it had a substance deserving of reverence. When perceptions, noticings, are governed by socially regulated repetition, images become harder than the sacred stones, and learning anything new harder than hell.

thought as movement

4

My intention is to describe some of the essential elements in Plato's conception of the educating processes, with a focus on thought-as-movement. However worthy the intention, I am struck by the irony of (1) preparing a set discourse on the movement of the dialectic method, and (2) striving for conclusions when my subject of concern is, roughly, inconclusiveness. With these difficulties in mind, I proceed.

Firm and constant commitment to education is exhibited throughout the Dialogues, and Socrates states the position strongly: " . . . so long as I draw breath and have my faculties, I shall never stop practicing philosophy and exhorting you and elucidating the truth for everyone that I meet" (*Apology* 29d; this and other translations are from *Plato: The Collected Dialogues* edited by Hamilton and Cairns [New York: Pantheon, 1961]). He goes on to chide his Athenian jury for giving "not attention or thought to truth and understanding and the perfection of (your) soul" (*Apology* 29e).

These three objects of attention (truth, understanding, perfection of soul) present an outline for the direction I wish to follow.

In Plato's view of knowledge, it is first necessary to conceive of the existence of truth, not *what* truth is, but *that* it is. On the belief that truth does exist, it follows that judgments may be made about the false as well as the true. For judgment to be valid and reliable in discriminating between true and false, the criterion (truth) must be fixed, eternal, unchanging, and absolute, beyond the everyday world of appearance. What is fixed, eternal, unchanging, and absolute is also pure, and to reach the pure one must employ the purest means possible. In *Phaedo* Socrates argues for the immortality of soul and in so doing places it beyond the temporal; in Book IV of the *Republic* and in *Timaeus* (69d, 70a) the soul is described as tripartite in nature (rational, courageous, and appetitive), with the rational part the highest good and the strongest. Hence the purest means to truth may be described as "reason moved by soul." The beginning of education in this framework is – following wonder itself – the application of reason, moved by soul, in the search for truth.

Second, this application must lead to some sort of understanding for there to be education. From the initial position *that* truth is, movement begins toward discovering *what* truth is. Coming to understand is partly a matter of divesting oneself of misconceptions. Nietzsche made the point when he said, "Convictions are more dangerous to truth than lies." Coming to understand begins with doubting all that has been believed to be true, including the reasons one has had for his beliefs. The first step in gaining knowledge is "knowing thyself," and this is begun by acquiring a knowledge of non-knowledge.

This first step of knowing oneself comes from the premise that everything known is known by someone – the knower. All persons have the power to select and reject things to be known and things to have faith in. This power of choice and decision, the personal judgment that is the final arbiter of questions, influences the character of knowledge. Knowing oneself then, means being aware of the processes of personal judgment and of how these processes affect the outcome of judgment, which is what we call knowledge. By choosing to be a certain kind of person, one also chooses to know certain things and deny other things. In the same way, by choosing to know certain things, one also chooses to be a certain kind of person. This reciprocity between the knower and the known is the starting point for understanding the limits of certainty and proof. At the end of *Theaetetus,* Socrates says, after failing to reach a conclusion on what knowledge is:

> . . . supposing you should ever henceforth try to conceive afresh, Theaetetus, if you suceed, your embryo thoughts will be the better as a consequence of today's scrutiny, and if you remain barren, you will be gentler and more agreeable to your companions, having the good sense not to fancy you know what you do not know. For that, and no more, is all that my art can effect . . . (210c).

Socrates expresses no distress at their failure to fix the notion of knowledge. Rather, he delights in the process of considering the question as exhaustively as he can. Rest is not a condition compatible with the philosophical nature living in Socrates, as evidenced by his insatiable wonder, his copious supply of questions, and his indefatigable energy for conversation (*Symposium* 223c-d).

Third, this very process is the work of "perfecting the soul."

Socrates' statement that wrongdoing or going to meet evil is always unintentional (*Protagoras* 358d) may be rephrased: Those who are not actively seeking the truth through reason drift unknowing toward evil or wrongdoing, which is the opposite of the true, the good, the right. If a man were confronted with a choice between ugliness and beauty, harm and well-being, evil and good, he would not intentionally choose the lesser benefit for himself. If a man is concerned for the truth, and is actively involved in finding it, he is also seeking the good, which is the highest activity of the soul. To realize this is to supply motivation for understanding truth, which is to say, for educating oneself.

I remember teaching a class of young Jesuit novitiates and being curious about how, at eighteen or nineteen, they could be so sure about what they were doing. I certainly wasn't able to make a commitment of such magnitude when I was that age, so I questioned them about theirs. The reactions to *my* doubt about *their* decisions were decidedly defensive at first. As we talked more about it, they began to see the real issue behind the question: if someone chooses to pursue what he takes to be truth, and if he has chosen correctly, then his choice will withstand the arguments against it, but if the choice is not entirely convincing to the chooser himself, he will be unable to examine it for fear of being wrong. We finally came around to understanding that the good or the true cannot be sought insincerely, and that my question really meant "how do you know that you are sincere?" I could tell from the looks on their faces when we uncovered this question that they were not only willing but anxious to consider it sincerely. In effect the question was being answered at that moment, without a word. At that point we shared a feeling, an energy among us, that was undeniably soulful and good.

I like the theme of motion because it coordinates in an intriguing manner with Plato's concept of the absolute. (At the same time I believe that an understanding of thought-as-motion-with-direction is almost a necessity for coming to grips with such elements of our own culture as the need for rules and limits, the affinity for completion, reliance on a final word or command, and the dislike of ambiguity – all symptoms of authoritarian behavior, and, in my view, all characteristics of American educational policy.)

Truth for Plato is eternal, unchanging, and absolute, a fixed goal; whereas certainty with regard to true knowledge appears to be unattainable, and knowing is essentially a *pursuit* with no end state. Socrates himself was never satisfied with his knowledge. He says in *Timaeus* (53d) that the ability to obtain final truth is God's, and his who is a friend of God, only. The "friend of God" I take to be a god himself, used here as an example to which men must aspire.

Men, however, can come to know the difference between opinion and knowledge; though knowledge is still undefined, we can know what it is not:

> But it is not, I am sure, a mere guess to say that right
> opinion and knowledge are different. There are few
> things that I should claim to know, but that at least is
> among them, whatever else is (*Meno* 98b).

The question now becomes: What is the best way to approach knowledge?

In *Phaedrus* Socrates says that "All soul is immortal, for that which is ever in motion is immortal" (245c). He goes on to explain that the soul is not moved, but as a first principle is a mover. This leads to a description of the "essence and definition of soul, to wit, self-motion" (245e). Through a nourishing example (itself an assumption), he then points out the proper application of this self-motion: " . . . as the mind of a god is nourished by reason and knowledge, so also is it with every soul that has a care to receive her proper food" (274d).

Plato regards the body (corporal life) as a hindrance to or restriction on the self-motion of the soul, which is directed toward a reunion with truth, recollected through the soul's existence before birth and found in a purer form after death. Death for Socrates is a healing, a recovery; in this sense, serious philosophers may "achieve" a partial death in life.

A strange doctrine for today. For Plato (or Plato's soul, wherever it moves), modern methods of sensory awareness exhilarate the body but corrupt the soul. They offer movement in the wrong direction. And the methods of experimental psychology are a mere playing with shadows. Strange.

So far three kinds of motion have been described. First, the philosopher's life is a process, a constant endeavour to reach the changeless truth that only God can possess finally; second, the soul, through which truth is sought, is in "self-motion," a process in itself; third, reason is moved and directed by soul, and since soul is self-motion, its product cannot be its opposite, rest (or in the sense of thought, conclusion). Rather, as in reincarnation, from the "conclusion" (the final rest or death of a thought) is generated a further question (new life). In terms of the soul-as-jar or sieve metaphor Socrates presents for Callicles (*Gorgias* 493b-c), a philosopher spends his life in "filling" the soul and repairing the "leaks." If his capacity for knowledge were fulfilled, life and thought would be of no further consequence. Knowledge is permanently acquired, but final knowledge of truth is not consonant with the condition of bodily mortality.

A philosopher thus occupies the precarious state of betweenness. His is the life between helplessness at birth and resolution at death (he has recognition of both sides); his is the activity between ignorance and knowledge, between mortality (human life) and immortality (freedom of soul). He seeks a partial death in life through knowledge of the true, the beautiful, the good. His love too is in a state of betweenness. Jaspers (1962, p. 155) elaborates on love (eros) by saying, " . . . love is like philosophy, a being-between. It is having and not having. It fulfills in nonattainment." Further, in *Symposium*, Plato has Diotima describe eros as " . . . halfway between mortal and immortal. A very powerful spirit, . . . and spirits, you know, are halfway between god and man" (202e). And later (204a), "Love is never altogether in or out of need, and stands, moreover, midway between ignorance and wisdom." This position is also that of the philosopher; with the knowledge of his ignorance, and the assumption that truth *is,* his life becomes energy spent (with reason as currency) in moving farther from ignorance, closer to truth. The sense of suspension in being "midway between ignorance and wisdom" implies movement with direction, and serves as grounds for disdain of the sophistic perch, the glib authority, the conclusion chosen with arbitrary and unjustifiable confidence. Eros clearly is an element, and a centrally important one, in the Platonic–Socratic conception of philosophy. Just as clearly, it has no place in sophistry.

Let me use Friedlander's remarks on the sexual element of

eros to lead into the final consideration of this chapter—
dialectical method.

Now, while a sexual element is—at least potentially—
always present in *Eros*, even the quest for truth and
the penetration to truth may for a moment, as in a
passage of the *Republic* (409a-b), be felt as an act of
begetting. Just as the begetter must be of the same
nature as the object of his love, so the lover of truth
must approach true being and touch it with that part of
the soul . . . which is akin to true being.
Insight and knowledge thus grow as part of one's
own existence, not separate from it (1958, p. 53).

The dialectic method may well have developed out of Socrates' "divine command" to find a man wiser than himself.
And what better way to find wisdom in a "wise man" than by
questioning him on what he knows? Just as insight and
knowledge grow as a part of one's existence, placing trust in
another person is a first step in self-affirmation. This self-
affirmation through trusted intercourse with another person
who will test those "convictions which are dangerous to
truth" is at once an opening or freeing of soul, and an act of
love. Friedlander lends support here, too, as he says that
"Plato also inherited the insight from Socrates that there is
no ready-made knowledge simply transferable from one person to another, but only philosophy *as an activity* [my ital-
ics] . . ." (1958, p. 166).

Sensory perception may act as a stimulus for rational consideration; for example, two contradictory impressions produce perplexity, a tension, which may be dealt with in at least

two ways: by a denial of one impression, or by an exacting consideration of the apparent differences to find a third or common element. Obviously, the second of these two possibilities is the one suited to dialectic.

The dialectic is begun with an examination of presuppositions in order to discover what is in question. Next, definitions are elicited to determine if two or more principles are in fact being confused as one. From here an hypothesis is put forth and tested in discourse in regard to potential conflicts between possible consequences (absurdities) and in regard to concomitance with perceived facts and/or with previously substantiated hypotheses, and finally in regard to concomitance with the highest conception of first principles, the cosmic order, truth, upon which the theory of knowledge is founded.

This description of dialectic presents, though incompletely, a pattern for inquiry, which ideally would lead to a knowledge of truth. As stated, the completion of this pattern is not essential for education to have occurred or for some knowledge to have been gained. The erotic involvement in the dialectical process—"to bring forth upon the beautiful with all one's soul"—*is* essential, for it is the living, active, trusting commitment to the *process* and *direction* of dialectic which is the root stem of education.

In the dialectic system, process and direction can be prescribed, but outcomes cannot. In a sense, then, dialectic is not a complete system, for one end of it, the outcome, is always open. Dialectic often has an aporetic end, an opening instead of a closure: the "head" on the body of dialectic is most commonly a refined question that might lead to a new inquiry.

Socrates deals with this point ironically in his request of Callicles:

> Well, they say it is not right to leave even tales
> unfinished, but we should fit a head on them, that they
> may not go about headless. Give us the rest of the
> answers then, that our discussion may acquire a head
> (*Gorgias* 505d).

Friedlander has suggested a list of seven "aporetic dialogues in search of a definition" (*Protagoras, Laches, Thrasymachus, Charmides, Euthyphro, Lysis, Hippias Major*). I would suggest as well that among the dialogues I am familiar with, *Theaetetus* and *Meno* are good examples of the aporetic, the open-ended, pathfinding, movement-producing theme which I have been trying to describe.

The pathfinding requires persistence and continual alertness to new directions. Socrates says in his final statement to Meno,

> On our present reasoning then, whoever has virtue
> gets it by divine dispensation. But we shall not
> understand the truth of the matter until, before asking
> how men get virtue, we try to discover what virtue is
> in and by itself (*Meno* 100b).

The initial perplexity, "can virtue be taught," has been elevated to a much higher perplexity, namely, whether or not virtue can be taught is a question of diminished import if virtue itself is not known. Jaspers (1962, pp. 126-7) puts it this way:

> When he seeks sharp definitions of universal concepts,
> Plato is not interested in relatively sound definitions
> of this and that; but by using their language to probe
> the idea of the absolute, beyond which no further
> advance or question is possible, he is seeking a
> language of the absolute itself. That is why all finite
> definitions end in impasse, perplexity. But in these
> perplexities the direction of the goal is sensed all the
> more acutely, though our ignorance of what it is
> becomes increasingly evident.

The refinement and sophistication of the perplexity, the hypothesis building and rebuilding is certainly a function, and perhaps the most important function, in dialectic. In fact, the purer the dialectical mode, the more likely an aporetic end.

Friedlander notes the "motif-like revival of the myth of Prometheus" in *Protagoras* which serves as a reminder that "cyclical closure" is one method of ending a dialogue rather than concluding it (1964, p. 32), and he goes on to agree with Jaspers (above) that the point of aporia is to make clear the goal and direction of the inquiry.

The notion of an investigation that does not lead to a clear stopping point is strange in a time when student papers and theses are expected to close with a final word, and semesters still end with a final test. The doctrines that Plato consistently returns to are equally strange. The three parts of the soul, the recollection of knowledge, and the primacy of an ideal world which our world of sense experience merely imitates are not seriously entertained in many classrooms.

Nonetheless, the love I feel for Plato leads me to ask what is of value in his mode of thought. One partial answer lies in the discontent that so many teachers feel, as if the teachers have within them some recollection of the way learning should be and as if the self-movement of their souls drives their reason toward some ideal of the communication and love that might exist between them and the students who come to them.

context and quality
in thought

5

Brief statements about thinkers are as tricky as brief statements about other humans. I would be unhappy to have my
character given a quick summary by someone else—I am
much too complicated and subtle and interesting for that.
Well-known thinkers must be equally unhappy to have their
lifework given summary treatment, although they, or their
ghosts, may be used to it by now. I will try to be fair to my
main subjects by examining specific aspects of their thought
and by using their own words quite often.

Epicurus, Plato, Kant, and computer scientists are among
thinkers who have worked toward certainty in their thought
by giving primacy to abstractions—to principles, procedures,
or categories that are entirely independent of particular
human experience. John Dewey and Albert Camus are among
those who have pointed to this severed connection of "certainty" and experience as the basal point for a novel pattern
of inquiry, analysis, and action in the world. Although these
two men are rarely spoken of in reference to each other, they
share a number of beliefs about man's condition and the na-

ture of thought. Both have undergone a radical gestalt switch in their perceptions, a refocusing of their attention from abstract rationalism to concrete experience as the proper beginning for thought about mankind. This gestalt switch has brought emphasis to two elements of human inquiry: the context of thought and the quality of thought.

As an introduction to a discussion of these two elements, it is useful to see how Dewey and Camus conceive the aim of philosophy. First, a sample of Dewey's statements:

> The purport of thinking, scientific and philosophic, is not to eliminate choice but to render it less arbitrary and more significant (1958, p. 30).

> The recorded scientific result is in effect a *designation* of a method to be followed and a *prediction* of what will be found when specified observations are set on foot. That is all a philosophy can be or do (1958, p. 36).

> . . . the significant business of philosophy is the disclosure of the context of beliefs . . . (1960a, p. 108).

> Philosophy, then, is a generalized theory of criticism (1958, p. xvi).

And from Camus's *The Myth of Sisyphus* (1955):

> Judging whether life is or is not worth living amounts to answering the fundamental question of philosophy (p. 3).

> There is but one truly serious philosophical problem, and that is suicide (p. 3).

> Reflection on suicide gives me an opportunity to raise
> the only problem to interest me: is there a logic to the
> point of death? (p. 7).

> Knowing whether or not one can live *without appeal*
> is all that interests me (p. 45).

The implications of these statements are of course numerous and diverse, but two related views emerge from the statements. One is the primacy of man's experience as a starting point for philosophy, and the other is the lack of any appeal to *a priori* reasoning. The first view is further supported by Dewey's saying that "if the finally significant business of philosophy is the disclosure of the context of beliefs, then we cannot escape the conclusion that experience is the name for the last inclusive context" (1960a, p. 108); and by Camus's stating that "if I ask myself how to judge that this question is more urgent than that, I reply that one judges by the actions it entails" (1955, p. 3). Further denegation of superexperiential reasoning is put forth with differing emphases but the same intent by Dewey:

> Nature *has* a mechanism sufficiently constant to
> permit of calculation, inference and foresight. But
> only a philosophy which hypostatizes isolated results
> . . . concludes that nature *is* a mechanism and only
> a mechanism (1960b, p. 248).

and Camus:

> I have never seen anyone die for the ontological argu-
> ment. Galileo, who held a scientific truth of great
> importance, abjured it with the greatest of ease as
> soon as it endangered his life. That truth was not

the worth at stake. Whether the earth or sun revolves around the other is a matter of profound indifference (1955, p. 3).

If we are to reject rational certainty through abstractions as the goal of thought, what are we to replace it with?

The answer begins with a revaluation of context. It is the neglect of such revaluation that Dewey calls "the most pervasive fallacy of philosophic thinking" (1960a, p. 92). The two fundamental parts to this fallacy, according to Dewey, are analysis and unlimited extension of universalization. The first part, he explains, is a result of elevating terminal elements of an investigation to the status of "final and self-sufficient," the logical conclusion of which is a doctrine of atomistic particularism that denies all connection and continuity. The second part comes about as a result of the presupposition that the universe is a single, coherent whole, and the assertion that the goal of thinking is to bring all things into that coherent whole. Both of these mistakes are the result of ignoring the limiting conditions which embrace any object of investigation and thought itself.

A second consideration in the revaluation of context involves the notion of event. Dewey does not doubt that all existences are *also* events, due to their temporal character, but that they are *only* events is a proposition which he feels can be maintained only by ignoring context. For him, an event is "both eventful and an eventuation." It is characterized by a "from which" and a "to which." These characteristics qualify any given event and make it distinctly the event which it is with a quality of its own. An event with a distinctive quality is no longer "only an event"; it becomes an object in its own right.

His third approach to context is centered on the matters of background and selective interest. Briefly, he considers both temporal and spatial aspects of background and comes to the conclusion that the whole contextual background can never come into question at once, with the corollary that something is always being taken for granted or is "understood." What he calls "selective interest" has been known by the more common philosophical term, "subjective," which, he says, is equivalent to individuality or uniqueness. He sees individuality as a "mode of selection which determines subject-matter."

These three considerations of context are by no means exhaustive, but without them or similar considerations any analysis of thought would be misleading. All thinking must take place in a context, and thinking about thought without reference to context, as Dewey puts it, "is in the end but a beating of wings in the void."

Camus proceeds from the truism that "All thought is anthropomorphic" to the statement that ". . . nostalgia for unity, that appetite for the absolute illustrates the essential impulse of the human drama. But the fact of that nostalgia's existence does not imply that it is to be immediately satisfied." In fact the tradition of what may be called "humiliated thought" is integral to human history. One reason for this is that man has imposed different forms of his own longing for clarity on a world that is not reasonable. What man has meant by "to understand" the world has really meant to reduce it to the human, "stamping it with his seal." The context in which man finds himself is an absurd one, born of the confrontation of his longing for clarity and the nonrational silence of the world.

The products of analysis and extension (as Dewey uses the

terms, that is, the final and universal) are essentially static in character, and for this reason Camus rejects them, as does Dewey. Further, Camus accepts the importance of "event" and of "background" and "selected interest." The reason for Camus's similarity to Dewey will become clear through an analysis of what Camus means by the absurd.

"Between the certainty I have of my existence and the content I try to give to that assurance, the gap will never be filled. . . . In psychology as in logic there are truths but no truth." This is in effect a statement of the impossibility of reaching final, self-evident, or universal conclusions. Placing himself in the context of the world as (in Dewey's terms) "brutely there," Camus says:

> I realize that if through science I can seize phenom-
> ena and enumerate them, I cannot, for all that,
> apprehend the world. Were I to trace its entire relief
> with my finger, I should not know any more. And you
> give me the choice between a description that is sure
> but that teaches me nothing and hypotheses that
> claim to teach me but that are not sure (1955, p. 15).

The terrible paradox that Camus perceives is that man has lucidity *and* seemingly definite walls around him; we are lucid enough to perceive the walls but we are unable to see a way out or even guess why the walls are there.

For Camus, the sole significant datum is the absurd, but it is not the world itself which constitutes the absurd. The absurd depends as much upon man as upon the world. To understand the world one must apprehend all of its events in all of their relations. This is impossible for, as Dewey suggests, the limits of man's knowledge due to the effects of context are finite, though indefinite. Nonetheless, as Camus vividly illustrates, there is in man a nostalgia, a wild longing for clarity, a need for familiarity, an appetite for certainty. "The absurd is essentially a divorce [between the man considering the world and the world considered]. It lies in neither of the elements compared; it is born of their confrontation." As such, the absurd is an event; it is a process, and it carries the same implications of qualitative relation to context as were mentioned above.

Camus himself is careful to say that he has not defined the absurd. Rather, he has given "an enumeration of the feelings that may admit of the absurd." Like Dewey's "background" and "selective interest," Camus's notion of the absurd is an understood quality which is not available for complete articulate definition, but is nonetheless effective in its very presence. He approaches it from many angles:

> In certain situations, replying 'nothing' when asked what one is thinking about . . . if that reply is sincere, . . . symbolizes that odd state of soul in which the void becomes eloquent, in which the chain of daily gestures is broken, in which the heart vainly seeks the link that will connect it again, then it is as it were the first sign of absurdity (1955, p. 10).

> At the heart of all beauty lies something inhuman, and these hills, the softness of the sky, the outline of these trees at this very minute lose the illusory meaning with which we had clothed them, henceforth more remote than a lost paradise. . . . that denseness and that strangeness of the world is the absurd (1955, p. 11).

> All the pretty speeches about the soul will have their contrary convincingly proved, at least for a time. From

this inert body on which a slap makes no mark the soul has disappeared. This elementary and definitive aspect of the adventure constitutes the absurd feeling (1955, p. 12).

I merely want to remain in this middle path where the intelligence can remain clear. If that is its pride, I see no sufficient reason for giving it up. . . . Perhaps this notion will become clearer if I risk this shocking statement: the absurd is sin without God (1955, p. 30). The absurd is lucid reason noting its limits (1955, p. 36).

From this perspective we have a picture of man as a stranger in a strange land, a stranger who is lucid enough to recognize this strangeness. Camus discusses three reactions to this confrontation: suicide, hope, and rebellion. Hope is closely related to suicide through a logical point. Ordinarily, it is hopelessness that is thought of in connection with self-annihilation. People pretend to believe that if a purpose or meaning of life cannot be proved or at least granted, then it necessarily follows that the opposite is true, namely, that life is not worth living. Camus points out that there is no common measure between these two judgments. Instead, the typical act of eluding direct confrontation with the matter-of-fact evidence of the absurd is that fatal evasion, hope (as mentioned in Chapter 1). For hope of another life one must develop the notion of "deserve" which presupposes the notion of justice for which there is no evidence even within experience, let alone nature; or one must fall prey to the trickery of those "who live not for life itself but for some great idea that will transcend it, refine it, give it a meaning, and betray it" (Camus, 1955, p. 7).

Another mistake is to suppose that the absurd dictates

death. Killing oneself amounts to confessing that life is too much and that one does not understand. But if there is no confessor and no relevant consequences of such a confession, what then is the point? To be laid low by a logical fallacy or conquered by a myth is no less absurd than the conditions which produced them. Nothing is gained save nothing.

"The absurd has meaning only in so far as it is not agreed to." And this is why Camus can say that "There is no fate that cannot be surmounted by scorn" (1955, p. 90). First understanding the absurd, then rebelling against it, scorning it, is an invitation to happiness. "I conclude that all is well," said Oedipus, and that remark becomes sacred:

> It echoes in the wild and limited universe of man.
> It teaches that all is not, has not been, exhausted. It
> drives out of this world a god who had come into it
> with dissatisfaction and a preference for futile suffer-
> ings. It makes of fate a human matter, which must
> be settled among men (1955, p. 91).

This could have come out of Dewey's *A Common Faith* (1934).

This discussion of context suggests quite naturally a comparison of Dewey's and Camus's notions about quality in thought: as an experience in a context, as an event, thought has a distinctly human quality. This quality is separable from thought only at the risk of arid and self-denying abstractions. It is worth juxtaposing Dewey's notion that experience is the last inclusive context available to philosophical analysis and Camus's statement, "At very most, (the absurd) mind will consent to use past experience as a basis for its future actions" (1955, p. 50). For the two thinkers, experience, context, quality, and thought appear to be interwoven in strikingly similar patterns.

At the end of *The Stranger* I sense an intense love of beauty, not because the narrative satisfies a longing for order and meaning, but because of its utter indifference. In Dewey's terms, I am experiencing a qualitative event which, because no meaning had been attached to it, is pervasive and "understood," though not yet an object of articulation. When Camus says, "Everything begins with lucid indifference," I am reminded of Dewey's statement that the only ontological given is a series of qualitative events which only come under scrutiny when they become problematic and provoke deliberate interaction. Before this, the events possess the denseness and strangeness of the world which was mentioned above in relation to the absurd. Camus provides a beautiful example of what Dewey has termed "the thinking of the artist; his logic is the logic of what I have called qualitative thinking";

> From the dark horizon of my future a sort of slow, persistent breeze had leveled out all the ideas that people tried to foist on me in the equally unreal years I then was living through. What difference could they make to me, the deaths of others, or a mother's love, or his God; or the way a man decides to live, . . . (1946, p. 152).

Qualitative thinking reflects the qualities of subjects, and these qualities can be articulated meaningfully only in context. Dewey warns that unless "underlying and pervasive qualitative determinations are acknowledged in a distinct logical formulation," intellectual analysis may be reduced to "a mechanical enumeration of isolated items or 'properties.'" In fact, "such intellectual definiteness and coherence as the objects and criticisms of esthetic and moral subjects possess is due to their being controlled by the quality of subject matter as a whole" (1960a, p. 180). Camus puts the same idea in more poetic if less precise terms: ". . . aspects cannot be added up. This very heart which is mine will forever remain indefinable to me" (1955, p. 14).

I can see a connection between the term "nostalgia" and what Dewey meant by "quality" when I read Camus's quasi-definition of thought, "Reason is an instrument of thought, not thought itself. Above all, a man's thought is his nostalgia" (1955, p. 36). And I am led to Dewey's main conclusion in his essay, "Qualitative Thought":

> . . . the immediate existence of quality, and of dom-
> inant and pervasive quality, is the background, the
> point of departure, and the regulative principle of all
> thinking (1960a, p. 198).

Although he says earlier (1960a, p. 184) that thought is "the operation by which (the problematic situation) is converted into pertinent and coherent terms," he realizes as does Camus that this effort in translation is itself a product of man's "nostalgia" for meaning and clarity which is itself a quality.

The last point I would like to make in this comparison is one concerning the mind-body relationship. It appears that Dewey and Camus agree in substance about the interconnectedness of mind and body. Dewey's two main arguments are: (1) an appeal to growth, the growth-process, as a series of connected phases of a continuity which underlies and is essential to both abstract notions of "mind" and "body"; and (2) an appeal to the "neglect of context fallacy" discussed above, through which consequences such as the minding behavior of an adult are mistakenly transformed into antecedent entities such as abstract "mind." These arguments are mutually dependent, for growth is the context of which Dewey speaks.

Camus's arguments emphasize the elusive maneuver of "the transcendental appeal to hope" as a basis for giving mind a substance of its own, the maneuver of "the body's judgment": "In a man's attachment to life there is something stronger than all the ills of the world. The body's judgment is as good as the mind's, and the body shrinks from annihilation. We get into the habit of living before acquiring the habit of thinking" (1955, p. 6). The example of Mersault's killing the Arab in *The Stranger* (1946) is relevant. The idea is that there are times when physical events alone are capable of influencing a man and making him act. It is not hatred, greed, envy, fear, or honor which makes Mersault kill the Arab, but simply the effect of the sun. His body reacts with his mind present: he did not "pull" the trigger, "the trigger gave way."

The essential similarity between these notions is twofold. First, neither Dewey nor Camus is willing to go outside the context in which he finds himself for knowledge or justification of any sort. Second, neither is willing to make an appeal to anything transcendental, not even nature itself, for man's condition. Ultimately, one's condition is one's own responsibility. The process we use for satisfying biological needs or nostalgia is a *transitive condition,* not an entity, of the body's relation to its context. This amounts to a transformation of the noun "mind" into the gerund "minding," which, due to the active implications, cannot be separated from the instrument of action, the body.

No matter how incomplete my comparison, the evidence is clear that the arbitrary distinction and separation of "existentialists" and "experimentalists" is not altogether justified.

Both Dewey and Camus seek to develop new patterns of inquiry and new emphases on qualitative details in man's experience. Many contemporary thinkers have joined in this task in full consciousness of a breakdown in the much honored assumption that "subjective" and "objective" are dichotomous. These thinkers are discovering and articulating a world which lies between the "subjective" and the "objective." In Polanyi's terms, they are minding the tacit dimension of personal knowledge.

overcoming
the art of obfuscation,*
or
the craft of clarity

6

Many people wish to remain obscure to hide suspected or actual incompetence, or to compensate for a lack of confidence in themselves. This practice in others is irritating and sometimes infuriating, especially when a straight answer to an important question is hidden; in ourselves, however, obfuscation is accepted because of its utility. It preserves an image of authority or status that we believe we surely deserve, but are unsure of.

Some academic disciplines breed obscurity. Much of American behavioral psychology, for instance, has achieved the rather dumfounding condition of being at the same time trite and inaccessible. The same may be said of American

---

*A confusing word that means "confusion."

positivist philosophy in relation to issues of human concern and human life: it is elaborately and positively irrelevant.

The principles of these two disciplines have effects on education, as well they might since it is not clear whether education is a discipline in itself or merely the executor of principles borrowed from other fields.

Behavioral psychology has given education an orientation toward efficient conditioning. The orientation has two sources. The first is a type of environmentalism derived from Locke's *tabula rasa* model of human minds. The idea is that minds are equally impressionable and that behavior is learned as a response to stimuli in the environment. The effectiveness of commercial advertising in this country owes much to the reactive-conditioning theories of Pavlov, Skinner, and followers of Freud. Educators who follow such theories aim to produce sameness in individuals through control of the environment. The egalitarian view that men are created with equal rights is then inverted to read that educators have the right to create men who will respond equally well to the same stimuli.

The second source is utilitarian theories of cost and reward. The idea is to reach goals with the least possible cost, energy, and time. These theories start from homeostatic drive-reduction concepts of behavior, concepts which assume that the natural state of organisms is rest and that the purpose of behavior is, if not death, at least leisure. Mass production industries are based on such theories. Although profit ratios are increased for management by utilitarian methods, there are serious question about the effects the methods have on the workers subjected to them. There are similar questions about the effects on students who work in mass production schools and who are at the same time the products of the school. The desired behavior in a cost-reward, utilitarian theory is a tightly conditioned pattern of reactive responses to a serial set of stimuli. Ideally, responses should become automatic, which is to say, immediate and unconsidered.

Just a word about positivist philosophy along with its recent mathematical formulations, as I don't know much about it. (I don't know much about it because in my brief encounters with those who are doing it I have been severely intimidated by their seeming intimacy with an abstract world that is no more than a puzzling game of arbitrary symbols in my world.) The only allowable statements are those that can be proved true or false, and only single, restrictive, denotative words (or symbols) can be used to make the statements. Metaphysics is out. Poetry is out. Love and suffering are out. Nonutilitarian ethics or morality is out. Personal and social character is out. History is out. The light is out.

Computer-assisted, and computer-monitored instruction are in (see Chapter 9). Curricula based on binary true-false, yes-no paradigms are in. Again the aim seems to be toward an environmental or utilitarian type of conditioning: get the whole crowd of us to respond equally well to the same controlled stimuli in the least time with the least effort. This method is also called (I don't think the irony is intended) "individualized instruction."

honoring obfuscation

These disciplines presently enjoy a certain deferential reverence-from-a-distance, an uncritical acceptance from outsiders. This deference comes not so much of understanding as it does from a willingness to praise those who make us feel ignorant. Confronted with one expert or another who proceeds to confound us with a speech or an article which doesn't appear to have anything to do with our own experience, we blame ourselves for not understanding. We shake our heads and assume that what was unintelligible was also right because an expert said it. We do this even when the expert states or implies rules for the conduct of our lives.

Experts are a plague to personal experience. These days we tend to pay much more attention to the internal consistency of certain theories than to their relation to our own experience. Experts and their theories are not harmful per se, for they are in the end only persons and ideas. It is the way we allow ourselves to be used by them that is harmful. *They* are the tools and *we* are the craftsmen, not the other way around.

There are two levels of confusion perpetrated by our rather unwarranted faith in experts and theories. The first is generated and sustained by our tolerance for jargon, which the American College Dictionary defines as: "unintelligible or meaningless talk or writing; gibberish." In translating jargon by substituting common synonyms for the special words, one often finds a pale point hardly worth making. Sometimes, by the same method, a good idea is uncovered that otherwise might have been missed completely.

The second level of confusion has to do with the influence of an attractive theory on men's images of themselves. We seem to have an unconquerable tendency for containing ourselves in a single metaphoric extension of an isolated theory. For example, we have had it proposed that:

Man is a system of electrons (biophysics)
Man is a computer (computer science)
Man is a soul (various theologies)
Man is an animal (biology)

Most current comparative psychology has proposed that man is a rat (echoes of the women's liberation movement?), or as Arthur Koestler puts it (1964, p. 560), ". . . for the anthropomorphic view of the rat, American psychology has traded in a rattomorphic view of man." Insofar as laboratory experimentation with animals has to do with learning theory, educators should be especially wary of what learning theories are good for and of what they imply. A person who adopts a theory of learning that is founded on laboratory experimentation with rats, pigeons, or monkeys, and restricts his teaching strategies to those prescribed by the theory runs the risk of doing great harm to the students he uses to ratify (in both senses) the theory. There are no data on a rat's feelings or on what he learns to expect from himself, from others, or from life. After laboratory animals learn their tricks, many are mad and all are destroyed.

The point is that a theory can distort and confuse men's images of themselves when the theory is lifted out of the context in which it was developed (see Chapter 5). We should have no hesitation in dropping a theory that has been applied to us when it no longer makes sense in terms of our lives. Rather than bend or ignore our own experience or mistrust our own feelings and intuitions to preserve a theory, we should refocus our attention on *the experience we are having and the persons we are having it with*. This, as I see it, is the intent and value of small group communications, a context-conscious activity which offers one means of breaking through the stupor induced by jargon – the jargon-language of feeling-less thinking and the jargon-behavior of theoretical living.

context and clarity

If there is one distinguishing quality of small group communications, it is a highly refined consciousness of the group as a context, a context which is the individual persons and their relations with each other. If there is one typical activity, it is practicing the craft of clarity, that is, trying to shake the habit of jargon in language and behavior. Thought of in this way, small group communications belong as much in the categories of philosophy and education as in the category of psychology. All three categories at different times emphasize the thing part of the world or the person part of the world or the relations between them. I believe that American behavioral psychology and positivist philosophy have emphasized the thing part at the expense of the person and the relations parts. Small groups are a means for confronting and correcting this overbalance.

The person part deserves attention because everything we do, including science, is influenced by personal values, assumptions, and presuppositions. It seems reasonable to explore and try to understand basic outlooks in ourselves and in others, especially when our values affect others, who in turn affect us. (A prime example of this reciprocity is the transaction between a teacher and a student.) I assume that clarity in personal relations leads to clarity in other activities undertaken jointly, such as dealing with a curriculum, establishing and abiding by regulations, and evaluating work done.

The values, assumptions, and presuppositions we have are sometimes called a frame of reference. Our frame of reference is the platform or the background of our perceptions. A person "responds, not to a given environment, but to what he takes to be the environment" (Thomas, 1968, p. 148). That goes for students *and* teachers: both need to know how the other is perceiving the environment they presumably share. Thomas goes on to say (p. 149):

> Where common knowledge is necessary for some joint enterprise . . . then a common frame of reference must be sought. But, on the other hand, there is no need to push a single frame of reference beyond the demands of the joint enterprise.

People do *not* need to think the same and be the same in order to work and learn together, but it is useful and perhaps necessary for them to understand each other's differences before they share a project effectively.

Two questions come up when people try to understand what they differ on and what they share. One is concerned with beliefs: What are my beliefs and what sorts of evidence will I accept as credible and relevant to their being right for me? The second deals with sincerity: Does my behavior truly express my beliefs; if not, would I rather change my behavior or my beliefs? A tremendous amount of learning and teaching (by example) comes out of considering just these two questions. They are an excellent prelude to and companion of any subject matter or curriculum that one intends to deal with. They are also implicit in small group processes.

There has been a good deal published about small groups in the last twenty-five years. As a body of literature it remains delightfully eclectic and shows signs of becoming even more so as it grows. Rather than try to make a summary of it in relation to the craft of clarity – a summary that might be too brief to be clear – I would like to deal with one model of small group processes which is not only elegant in its simplicity, but which makes the most sense in relation to my experience with small groups.

the johari window

The Johari Window is a graphic model of awareness in interpersonal relations, conceived in 1955 by Joseph Luft and Harry Ingham ("Johari" is pronounced "Joe-Harry"). The model is most fully explained in Luft's two books, *Group Processes* (1963; 2nd ed., 1970) and *Of Human Interaction* (1969).

Graphically, the model is a square divided into four quadrants which represent the proportion of information about a person that is (1) open in that it is known both to self and to others; (2) blind in that it is known to others but not to self; (3) hidden in that it is known to self but not to others; and (4) unknown in that it is known neither to self nor to others. From any one person's point of view, the model looks like this:

	Known to self	Not known to self
Known to others	1 Open	2 Blind
Not known to others	3 Hidden	4 Unknown

The object of interaction between persons or between groups of persons is usually to enlarge the open area (Q1) and thereby diminish Q2, Q3, or Q4. The blind area (Q2) is reduced by accepting information from others; the hidden area is reduced by offering information to others; and the unknown area is reduced primarily by after-the-fact confirmation of previously unconscious or preconscious information in the forms of motivations, defenses, impulses, and the like. As Luft points out, the area of Q4 cannot be known and therefore cannot be represented with any accuracy by line boundaries. This is also partially true of the blind and hidden quadrants. But if the model is seen as a representation of the *quality* of awareness among people rather than as a representation of the *quantity,* its lack of precision is not important.

The quality of awareness among people must be evaluated in terms of the mixture of all four quadrants that is satisfactory to the people in specific contexts. Greater openness is desirable only when it contributes to a more satisfactory balance of transaction with others. For instance, if I spend some of my attention and energy trying to protect a certain bit of information from somebody who already knows it, I am wasting effort that could be put to more satisfactory use. If this person and I are able to discover what is happening, or if a third person can point out how our partial blindness of each other is inhibiting further understanding, the information frees us. It leads to a better quality of transaction, which in turn leads to a higher level of sharing.

The following is an abbreviated description of the seven qualities that Luft outlines (1969, pp. 6-8) as an introduction to the Johari Window.

1. The model begins by considering consciousness (what is felt within oneself) and awareness (what is felt outside oneself) simultaneously. These states of knowing are central to any consideration of human interaction.

2. Intrapersonal and interpersonal affairs are inextricably united. They can be considered together in the Johari framework without violating any particular theory of personality.

3. The model is essentially content free. Any number of assumptions about the sources of human behavior may be applied within it, while the structure of the model maintains a focus on various states of awareness and consciousness.

4. The constructs implicit in each of the quadrants lend themselves to verification. Even the unknown quadrant is *eventually* confirmable.

5. The model can be applied to any human interaction. There is no inherent subject limitation.

6. The model is sufficiently uncomplicated so that it is readily used. One does not need extensive background in the behavioral disciplines to grasp the model and use it.

7. The processes inherent in the model guide the reader to important characteristics of human interaction. The significance of any interpersonal event is sharpened when it is seen in the context of all four quadrants. In other words, as one quadrant changes size, at least one other will also change size, and the proportions of the whole will be altered.

The thing that strikes me about these qualities is their strictureless structure. The model is a scheme of good sense that is most accommodating to laymen and professionals alike. It is a remarkable example of organization without rigidity (see Chapter 13); it is an attempt to focus on contextual truths instead of absolute answers, and on sharing frames of reference under conditions that encourage consent rather than control.

Implicit in the model is a concern for the processes of change—changing perceptions, changing awareness, and learning. Though the concept of change is perhaps *the* basic concept of all human life, a fact of every moment's existence, it is resisted in principle by some. My guess is that we think change is "good" when we feel a part of it and "bad" when we feel subjected to it. Of course there are some people who believe that they don't really have much to say about changes in the world, and just let it be.

Luft (1970, p. 15) has outlined some principles of change on which the processes of the Johari model are based:

1. A change in any one quadrant will affect all other quadrants.
2. It takes energy to hide, deny, or be blind to behavior which is involved in interaction.

3. Threat tends to decrease awareness; mutual trust tends to increase awareness.

4. Forced awareness (exposure) is undesirable and usually ineffective.

5. Interpersonal learning means a change has taken place so that Q1 is larger and one or more of the other quadrants has grown smaller.

6. Working with others is facilitated by a large enough area of free activity. And increased Q1 means more of the resources and skills in the membership can be applied to a task.

7. The smaller the first quadrant, the poorer the communication.

8. There is universal curiosity about the unknown area, but this is held in check by custom, social training and diverse fears.

9. Sensitivity means appreciating the covert aspects of behavior, in quadrants 2, 3, and 4, and respecting the desire of others to keep them so.

10. Learning about group processes as they are being experienced helps to increase awareness (enlarge Q1) for the group as a whole as well as for individual members.

11. The value system of a group and its membership may be noted in the way *unknowns* in the life of the group are confronted.

12. A centipede may be perfectly happy without awareness, but after all, he restricts himself to crawling under rocks.

These principles are strong in their cooperative and contextual emphases, and they are consistent with a faith that people are in fact capable of dealing with their own problems and desired changes, given the opportunity to do so. This faith implies a rather unique view of a leader's function, be he called a small group facilitator or a classroom teacher. The function is to help provide the conditions that will encourage the members of the group to take on responsibility for their own leadership, their own decisions, and the refinement of the processes in which they are engaged. On this point, Richard Farson has some good things to say (1969):

> Instead of looking to a professional elite for the solution to any social problems, look to the greatest resource available – the very population that has the problem. Many of us tend to have a low opinion of people, those wretched masses who don't understand, don't know what they need or want, who continually make mistakes and foul up their lives, requiring those of us who are professionally trained to come in and correct the situation. But that is not the way it really works. The fact is that some drug addicts are much better able to cure addiction in each other than are psychiatrists; some convicts can run better rehabilitation programs for convicts than do correctional officers; many students tend to learn more from each other than from many professors; some patients in mental hospitals are better for each other than is the staff. Thousands of self-help organizations are doing a good job, perhaps a better job at problem solving than is the profession that is identified with that problem. People who have the problems often have a better understanding of their situation and what must be done to change it. What professionals have to do is learn to cooperate with that resource, to design the conditions which evoke that intelligence.
>
> . . . .
>
> In this way society can be truly self-determining and self-renewing. The special beauty of this formulation

is that it fits the democratic goal of enabling the people to make a society for themselves. Mankind can rely on people as a resource for much more than is possible to imagine. It's really quite difficult to find the ceiling of what people can do for themselves and each other, given the opportunity.

Establishing the conditions which allow for this type of democratic participation in change is not simple. The leader must decide not to lead in traditional ways, and the group members must learn to overcome their expectations of what leaders are supposed to do. We have long experience in relying on leaders and authorities of one sort or another for the final word in questions of responsibility and decision-making, and it takes a *new experience* to be able to understand that another kind of responsibility, shared responsibility, is in fact possible and effective. Some of the problems a leader and a group have with "nondirective" leadership are explored in Chapter 8.

The experience of change can be clarified by examining the Johari model in detail. The open quadrant (Q1) represents awareness that is shared by self and others. By definition, then, at any given moment of interaction between two persons their Q1 areas will be equal and congruent. They will contract (through various forms of forgetting) and expand (through new information offered and accepted) in direct proportion to each other. The open quadrant is the only one whose size is determined jointly by self and other; it is the only one in which conscious sharing occurs. "To realize its existence, especially in relation to the other quadrants which are not open in one manner or another, is to establish an aspiration, if not a direction, for change" (Luft, 1969, p. 18). Luft goes on to say (p. 18):

The greatest single source for acquiring more openness is in the matrix of relationships to oneself and to others. Because each of us has, through experience, acquired some "trained incapacity" in functioning in this matrix, I believe that there is a genuine need to find interpersonal experiences which lead to more openness to the world. . . . indiscriminate or forced openness is neither useful nor desirable. Effective openness, however, takes work and some boldness . . .

One of the reasons it takes boldness has to do with the blind area, Q2 (Luft, 1969, p. 27):

Having blind spots about my own behavior means that I am eternally vulnerable to others. Knowing I am blind or partially blind helps a great deal, but does not resolve the dilemma. Knowing others have blind areas helps a bit more, but still does not remove the predicament.

We can never know all there is to know about ourselves; a whole person is such an amazingly complex thing, constantly changing and constantly growing, that it is impossible to be conscious of everything that is going on at any given moment. Others can perceive things in and about us that we ourselves cannot, at least not without some help. One question about Q2 blindness is how much we *want* to know about the way others see us. There is a whole world of information in the perceptions of others, there for the asking, but withheld by them out of a sense of tact, diplomacy, or even a desire to manipulate. Knowing more about how others see us, about how we affect others without intending it, does not necessarily mean that we will change what we do or the way we are. It does mean, however, that future *misunderstandings* related to a previously blind or inadvertent effect will be reduced. Our confusion about how we are "coming across" can undermine the best of intentions. For example, a shy person who finds it difficult to offer his thoughts without being asked and who tries to appear congenial and "askable" by smiling pleasantly in silence could be perceived as aloof and conceited. A single first impression such as this could unnecessarily postpone any sort of communication between him and those who misperceive him. Being blind to the reasons for the effects he is producing, the shy person remains alone in the dark.

It is often rather hard to deal with unsolicited perceptions of our blind spots. In the first place we are usually surprised, and in the second place we resent somebody who thinks he sees through us. On the other hand, it is often an illuminating and exciting experience to ask for help in understanding our effects on a context when we feel things aren't just right or when we feel misunderstood. Other people are usually willing to give their perceptions when they are asked, and they are almost always informative. Asking for help is sometimes hard because we all know there are things about ourselves that are difficult to face. I think it is worth the risk, though, for the alternatives—(1) perpetuating unintended behavior that keeps us separated from others and (2) persisting in the habit of *blaming others* for misunderstanding us—are grievous, oppressive, and wastes of time.

There is a close connection between Q2 and the hidden area, Q3. For instance if another person were to offer his perception of something you do but are unaware of doing, he would be unhiding part of himself in order to unblind part of you. In one sense he is giving you a gift of part of himself.

There is certainly risk in that sort of gift giving because it is so personal and it stands the chance of being rejected. If it is accepted, however, the recipient may well feel a desire to return the gift in kind. Through the interaction of Q2 and Q3, the open area is enlarged. Sharing occurs.

Another dynamic of the opening of your hidden area is a sort of spontaneous remission in the other person's blind area or perhaps in his unknown area. This happens, I think, because part of his understanding of you is relating what you are saying to his own experience. In doing so, new dimensions of his old experiences are likely to become clear, perhaps for the first time, because they are looked at in a new way, from a new context. This reciprocal process is sometimes startling in its swiftness and in the amount of learning that it produces. The richness of meaning in this experience of shared learning, no matter how much "hard work and boldness" are involved, is unequivocal. It is usually remembered with joy.

For the most part you are in charge of disclosing what is hidden (in Q3) about yourself. As Luft points out (1969, pp. 56-7):

> What you reveal is pretty much up to you, though not
> entirely so. Sometimes pressure from conflicting
> forces in all the quadrants forces accidental disclosure.
> Slips of the tongue, unusual associations of thought,
> and all kinds of mistakes may occur which reveal
> what you don't want to reveal. It takes energy, atten-
> tion, and perhaps a good imagination to do an able job
> of hiding. Not disclosing could be a form of lying,
> obliquely by an act of omission. Selective disclosing
> could do a fine job of misleading, too.

Again, the model does not imply total openness or self-disclosure as a goal, but rather a balance of disclosure and discretion. "Disclosing too much creates at least as many problems as disclosing too little – but of a different kind. Strict control over Q3 disclosure tends to create distance in relationships. Lax control means relationships either too close (smothering) or too demanding" (Luft 1969, p. 57). There is no way to prescribe a formula for this balance. It is a matter of personal judgment and intuition. I would guess that each of us has a *desired* balance somewhat different from the one we find ourselves in now. The Johari model makes it clear that something can be done about such a desire if people are willing to work together to make it into a real experience instead of leaving it as a real fantasy.

In any case it is impossible to be totally open as long as there exists an unknown area in you, and inevitably there is much unrealized potential and many forgotten experiences in each of us. How and when these unknowns come into consciousness is less a matter of will than of a receptive attitude to new contexts, new experiences, and your own intuitive feelings.

Though I don't deny the importance of the unknown or unconscious part of our personalities, I don't have much interest in approaching it historically or focally, as would a psychoanalyst. This is a bias on my part (shared by Lewin, Rogers, Perls, Laing, and Luft, among others), but I think that what is important in the unknown area will make itself apparent in the present in ongoing experiences, feelings, thoughts, and expectations, and in the way we understand our immediate problems. Our primary task is to become as aware as possible of what we are doing now; as we become more aware, the relevant parts of our unknown area will make themselves known. I would rather tramp after Zorba and share his vitality in encountering vitality itself than lie down in Freud's chamber and tiptoe backward into the shadows.

a valuable waste
of time

7

Recently I learned something from braving what I considered a bad situation, and I would like to share it with others who are involved in human relations work – teaching, administrating, or facilitating small group communications.

Since 1967 my colleagues and I have been planning, organizing, and conducting small group communication experiences for people who work in public education. We maintain contact with the participants in our program for at least one year through a series of meetings which vary from three days to two weeks in length. Until recently I had never met with a group for less than three days, and I had assumed that it takes at least that much time to establish conditions for a lasting and meaningful experience – something more than a warm and fading memory.

A friend of mine who knew a little about our work asked me to start off his training program for school planners with "some personal communications." I was leary of the schedule: meet the planners Sunday night; do an hour's worth of "input" Monday afternoon; have an informal group session Monday night. Most of Monday was to be spent listening to a relay team of specialists in facilities planning. Had he not been my friend, I would have refused. But he was my friend.

There were only nine participants, all men. Six were employed on the assistant or associate superintendent level by six different school districts, and three were businessmen who did contract work in school planning. Sunday evening, as we were leisurely inquiring about one another's interests and the like, it became obvious that every one of these men was concerned about "the community." They each saw implicit and in some cases explicit divisions between the school administration which they represented and the community which the administration was supposed to represent. They did not appear to be as concerned about the irony of this situation as they were about the difficulty they had in convincing the community that it was getting what it needed from the schools. Since most of these men represented urban districts, I inferred the "community" to mean the poor minorities who constitute the majority of urban populations. With this in mind I went to bed wondering what to do the next evening. I had two or three hours to deal with the problem and all its implications, and I knew that lack of time was a big part of the problem itself – spending only a few hours here and there in meetings with the community and coming away even more rankled because of the hostile frustrations that inevitably raise their fists and pound the meetings to a close. "Community relations" is a euphemism for race relations: racism. Good guys and bad guys: negotiators and militants. How shall I

spend two hours with nine white men who considered themselves good guy negotiators having a hell of a time fending
off the bad guy militants?

That is the bad situation. Below is a description of what
happened and why I tried what I tried.

doings

For twenty minutes before the meeting I sat outside and
watched a gang of young looking clouds cruising around in-
differently, forming transient cliques, swarming into pictures
and dissolving, not giving a damn for what I wanted them to
do. Then the planners came.

Inside, I explained that this was an unusual task for me,
that I wasn't used to working in this sort of situation, and that
I had no intentions of trying to help form a "small group" in
such a short time. (Several of the men were very sensitive
about "sensitivity training" and were visibly relieved to hear
this.) I went on to say that I thought we might pursue their
concerns about community problems since that was one thing
we all had in common. That was agreeable. (At this point I
was struggling to overcome my experience in organically
structured [non-structured] groups which was begging me to
just let things evolve and stop playing the leader. But I knew
that there simply was not enough time. The things we do for
friends.) Go.

I said that I was going to set up an artificial situation by
stipulating two rules: (1) If we could not talk about something

that was happening at the present time, inside this room, then we would remain silent; no talk about the past, the future, or about persons outside the room would be allowed. (2) Whenever we spoke we would address ourselves to one other person and look him in the eyes while we were speaking; talking to the group in general (as I was doing then) or talking to oneself would not be allowed. With remarkably well-controlled enthusiasm the group agreed to try this experience.

At this point we all lapsed into a silence which was interrupted by intermittent chuckling and shuffling. As a number of brows began to furrow in puzzlement and heads began to swivel in search of some visible topic to begin with, the inevitable jokes were trotted out. The first one was about a Mississippi Baptist minister trying to drown a prostitute. The laughter was rather forced. Several one-liners were flicked out. They fell into the uncomfortable air that grew around us. The man who told the joke began to explain that he had been born in the North, and although he had lived in the South for fifty-one years he was an "integrationalist," and held no prejudice. He added that as the oldest man there, he "was ready to argue with anyone in the room," whereupon, lacking an opponent, he launched into his opinion of long hair and the inherent virtues of the comb. The rest of us were baffled.

I had reminded him that his joke was outside the rules, but now I was waiting for someone else in the group to remind him that his discourse was prerecorded and therefore not of the present. Two or three people tried to ask him what he was talking about. He looked at me and asked if I would make these people stop interrupting him. I considered it and said that I would not. This remark precipitated the most intense and sudden fury that I have seen in a long time. I tried to clarify the man's response with questions about what had angered him so. (Had I not kept him engaged at that point he would have walked out of the room red-faced and puffing and cursing.) He had taken my remark as an insult, as another way of saying "shut up." I replied that he had requested me to tell others to "shut up" and that I had refused, not wishing to tell anyone that. We came to a stuttering peace and he stayed with us.

This incident lapsed into another silence which was eventually ended by two of the men saying that they had been offended by the joke and that they felt uncomfortable about the outburst. I asked to know more about these feelings, mainly to give the "offender" a chance to be understood and to understand what had happened, but the men folded their arms and refused to enter further discussion. I will not describe what went on for the next hour or so except to say that the most popular topic was the impossibility of talking about the present. I tried asking several of the men what they were *feeling* at a given moment; they responded by telling me what they were *thinking*. When I persisted by pointing out the discrepancy between what I had asked for and the response I was getting, I received cross looks, sighs, and shrugs.

When things were really dragging and my energy for maintaining the rules had been exhausted, my suggestion that we stop this foolishness was met with new smiles and long awaited stretching.

There was much talk about this being a boring, wasteful meeting. There was a little curiosity about what it all meant and a unanimous appeal for adjournment to the bar. I used my position as leader once again and asked for just a few more minutes. I wanted to explain why I had done this aggravating thing to them, instead of giving a nice lecture or a slide presentation.

mindings

In a broad sense what I had done was structure a situation analogous to the sort of school-community meetings that these men had participated in time and again. It was a demonstration of manipulation without force—a form of middle class militance, if you will. Sneaky, artificial, effective, and maddening. I ran the meeting, I determined what we would talk about, and I enforced David's Rules of Order. I was the administrator and they were the community. After all, I was the resident expert, right? I had the right, right? These men had come to the meeting because they wanted to find out what I was up to, what I had to say for myself—much like concerned parents who want to know what their local experts in education are up to and what they have to say for themselves. The first thing officials do in that sort of meeting is make a statement about the rules for discussion; here I had made the rules and they had felt obligated to accept them. I went one step farther, though, and *admitted* that my rules were artificial.

My rules demanded a very basic change in the planners' language and perception before anything at all could be said. I was demanding that the planners stop using their language and begin using mine. If they would use my language, I would listen. Otherwise I would rule them out of order. They learned quickly that I had posed an extremely difficult task and it generated a surprising amount of deeply personal resentment. They had a lot they wanted to talk about, but I wouldn't let them. They couldn't figure out how to use my language; soon they didn't even *want* to figure it out, and finally they began to express their frustration by calling the whole thing a waste of time and by challenging my competence. If they weren't so experienced in putting up with some authority or other, however frustrating, they would have walked out.

I think that their deeply felt personal resentment at not being able to use their own language was the most dramatic point made through the experience. Language is a very personal possession. People are judged by it. These even-tempered, well-dressed professionals really got mad at me. I wanted them to *feel* the anger and to feel the control it demanded of them so I could make the next point without fear that they would forget it the next day.

The language they couldn't use, the language about the present, is a "whole person" language which is basically a feeling language. A person always has a feeling at a given time; he may not have a cogent thought to go with it, but he always has a feeling. When he is able to recognize the feeling, accept it, and express it in words or movement, then thoughts and feelings merge. Thoughts alone make a "head" language which comes on cold (mistakenly termed "objective" by its protectors) and often domineering or pompous. Men like the planners use a "head" language in their work most of the time, and they use it (because they are "professionals" after all) when confronting the community. They know it separates them from the community and exemplifies their status – and that's why they use it.

The "community," the nonprofessionals, the people of the neighborhood streets (and all children) often use a "whole person" language where feelings and meanings and expression and thought are all together. This language is vital, personal, idiosyncratic, poetic, sincere, explosive, compassionate. It reveals the concerns of the person using it. (This is a point about language and not a characterization of the people who use it. Whole person language can be employed to shuck and hustle just as "head" language can, but it is more difficult to use that way in person.) "Head" language separates the person from what he is saying. Otherwise it could not be "objective." I was trying to nudge these men into the language that their communities often use, hoping that such an experience would make it easier for them to at least understand the difference between "head" and "whole person" language.

The experience, then, had two major points: (1) I wanted to demonstrate what happens to someone when another person demands that he follow certain language rules in order to speak. These men make such demands on their community people all the time without knowing it, and it makes the community people mad, just as I made these men mad. (Teachers do it to kids, too.) (2) I wanted to demonstrate that although the voiced opinion was that the meeting was "a waste of time," a great deal of inadvertent learning occurred. Who, for instance, was responsible for the use of our time? How easy was it for me to manipulate the others to the point of anger so I could then say something like "I tried, but you know, I just can't talk to these people – all they do is get mad"?

After I had talked about rules and language and anger, the participants began to expand these points into their own experience. The thing that pleased me most was their discovery that a lot of the confusion and bitterness between themselves and the community was *not* so much a difference in aspirations or goals for the improvement of schools as it was a difficulty in sharing a means of expressing these aspirations and goals. They began to explain to each other that two people who wanted the same things could very easily end up accusing each other of wanting opposite things simply because they were unable to understand each other's language. Further, they made the connection between this experience and the common experience of teachers and students in so-called learning situations.

The final thing I wanted to make clear was the difference between *experiencing* the problems we had been talking about and merely being informed about them. They had heard presentations that very morning which they couldn't remember, but, I said, I was willing to bet anyone in the room that he would not forget this "presentation" because he had been emotionally a part of it. No takers.

I continue to prefer longer experiences with small groups, and I do not know how well my brief method would work with a different group in a different context. I do know that the method was powerful when I used it, and it could be powerful again. The problem in using it, of course, is contextual, as with any other method. Its main value is in dealing with perhaps the most common contextual problem: time.

one small group leader: paradoxical problems of becoming a member of his own group

8

During the last twenty years the small group context, as a means for management training, task achievement, therapy, academic learning, and many forms of personal growth, has been subjected to the rack of scientific investigation. The character of published information on small groups (under many aliases) has become more and more that of the formal research report. The study of small groups now has a certified place in several fields of social science, and as a consequence of the empirico-scientific measurement paradigm assumed by most social scientists, the nature of the information sought and reported is naturally skewed toward controllable, statistically analyzable unit variables. One of these "unit variables" is thought to be the group leader, and because his variations are defined restrictively for research purposes, some questions about his place in the group have virtually been ignored.

In the medley of information now available to us about small groups there are only a few notes about the problems a group leader has in becoming a *member* of his group, if he wishes to do so. We usually read either about techniques available to him for manipulating circumstances to produce desired effects or about differences between "leaderless" groups and "led" groups. Both techniques and categories of leadership are viewed in light of the concept of leader effectiveness, derived from functional role theory.* The basic question was then and remains now: What is the relationship between leader behavior and group performance?

Some of the ideas that go with this question help in understanding why *membership* as a focus of inquiry is reserved for group participants and not for group leaders. Generally the leader's *membership* in the group is not considered at all. His *role* takes the attention of investigators. When his membership is considered, it is in terms of *acceptance,* which is tacitly equated with membership. Acceptance relates to the key notion of effectiveness.

It is my view that becoming an accepted leader, which I see as a role function, is to be distinguished from becoming a group member, which I see as a transactive quality; moreover, I feel that a leader has more difficulty than a "registered participant" in becoming a member. Very briefly, the situation I wish to explore is this: at the beginning of a group the leader is automatically in the group by virtue of his role as a leader,

---

*The prototype study in this area is often considered to be Lewin, Lippitt, and White's work of 1940 on "Leader Behavior and Member Reaction in Three 'Social Climates,'" as reported in Cartwright and Zander's *Group Dynamics* (1967).

but he is out of the group as a person-in-himself by virtue of the same role (which is assigned to him by the participants, either in compliance with or against his wishes). To be in the group as a person, he must be ousted from the group as a leader: re-entry into the group following this ouster assists the leader in becoming a member.

Let me sharpen some terms. I am thinking mainly about "growth" groups, as opposed to "task" or "training" groups, and about "leaders" who are interested in their own involvement in groups more than in merely overseeing the involvement of others. I am motivated by a desire to better understand what has happened to me in groups over the last few years, rather than by an ambition to establish a theory about small group dynamics with regard to leadership. I will be grateful if this chapter is not mistaken by the reader as a prescriptive declaration, but taken instead for what it is intended to be – a description of personal involvement in a certain context which I believe has implications for many types of personal doings and dealings in other contexts, such as "teaching" in classrooms.

Perhaps the best way to begin is with a definition of group membership. This is unfortunate because I can't do it. The second best way may be to explain why I can't begin in the best way. I know what membership is in much the same way that I know what love is. This sort of knowing is felt more than cognized. I know membership or love every time it happens, and I know it with a certainty which simply cannot be overcome by attempts to prove it false. Just as surely, I know when membership or love that was certain at one time is *not* happening anymore. No one who has experienced loving or being loved can reasonably deny that such experience exists, no matter what name he gives the experience. Poets, philosophers, psychologists, and mothers have tried to define love so those who haven't experienced it could understand it. The definitions fall short. There is in all of us who thought we knew what love was before we felt it sufficient conviction later that we really didn't know what to expect. Moreover, we are helpless when we do know to explain it fully to others, much less to define it. So it is with membership. I could try forever to define it and perhaps always be right, but I'd never be done and therefore, in the end, the "definition" would be misleading. I can suggest that group membership is like love; it is a pleasure and an honor, it is altogether a good feeling, and it is important.

I am *not* trying to suggest that the phenomenon of membership is incapable of being induced and shared among many. Rather, it is a superverbal phenomenon which has its potence and meaning *in a context*. Since the context of its occurrence and growth cannot be fully recreated through language (though it can be abstractly represented), the phenomenon itself cannot be completely reproduced verbally, either.

Even though I cannot define it, I can describe membership with some validity if I consider it as an object in its own right, that is, as an event-in-context. Membership has an object status by virtue of a general characteristic of events that Dewey (1960) elucidates in his revaluation of context. His argument, briefly, is this: All existences are *also* events, by virtue of their temporal character, but that they are *only* events is a position that can be maintained only by ignoring context. His position is that an event is both "eventful and an eventuation." It is characterized by a "from which" and a "to which." These characteristics qualify any given event and make it distinctly the event which it is with a quality of its own. An event with a distinctive quality is no longer *only* an event; it becomes an object in its own right.

The context that concerns me is small "growth" groups, and the "from which" elements of this context give me a starting point for a discussion of leader membership.

Four conditions are necessary for membership to occur. I will discuss these four roughly in their own natural sequence: they would never, of course, appear in isolation in the experience of a leader. The conditions are: submission to anonymous authority, trust, risk, and acceptance.

Before proceeding, I would like to describe in more detail the type of group leader for whom membership is a problem. There are essentially two modes of leadership commonly found in current practice. The first is the *model* mode wherein the group leader will assume the role and posture of the ideal member as he conceives the animal. He will demonstrate the ideal by acting out what he expects of each participant in terms of group behavior. The idea is that perfect imitation will produce another living model—an idea at the foundations of certain religious institutions, Bandura's theory of social learning, and many phases of military life. In this model the leader is seen primarily as a teacher and only secondarily, if at all, as a learner. This type of leader would not necessarily want to become a member of his group in the sense I have in mind; therefore, this discussion is not directed toward him.

The other mode is one that may be referred to as *scanning*. In this mode, the leader may unconsciously be acting as a model, but his intention is to facilitate and encourage everyone in the group to scan (through interaction) the persons and

the attitudes present in order to construct an eclectic indige-
nous model for all to understand. The model is a product of
the group's efforts, rather than a product of the leader's experience alone. This mode is akin to the Socratic and experimental methods of philosophy, and to the fundamental
starting point of existential thought, namely, that philosophy
begins with an experience of the whole person rather than
with the products of sensation, cognition, or affect in isolation.
In this mode it is difficult to distinguish the teacher from the
learner, and it is to this type of leader that membership is an
issue.

submission to anonymous authority

From the moment a commitment is made to attend a group,
a client-professional situation is produced. There is the one
who comes and the one who is come to. The mere presence of
a leader is a fulfillment of the expectation for authority. The
assumptions which experience provides, that when something is organized it is controlled and that what is controlled
has a controller, are packed up and brought along without a
second thought. When the leader is introduced, these expectations are secured; that he is the leader is learned immediately, though his name may fade out of mind in thirty seconds.

Generally, the first thing a leader says to the group is that
he does not want to be a leader, but a participating observer,
as he hopes all of the group will become. He will deny that he
wants power over the group. It is significant to note that no
one else in the group has any cause to make such a humble

statement. The trainer becomes a gift-giver, he offers his status, and by so doing he creates suspicion, discomfort, bewilderment, scorn, and other varied reactions in the gift-getters. Rarely is there gratitude in return for this gift, as it is seen more in terms of abnegation than generosity or respect.

The fact of his being accepted as *a* leader is unavoidable, but he may become an unacceptable leader with whom the group feels stuck. Because expectations developed by most people over a lifetime lead them to seek behavior-clarifiers in new situations, and because group leaders are commonly reluctant to provide overt satisfaction for these expectations (one of the things to be learned in a group is how to decide on and develop one's own preferences in behaving), model needs arise. The leader offers no verbal information as to what "proper" behavior is, so people seek covert information in the behavior of a perceived model who is usually the leader, the old-timer.

Model needs are quite high at the beginning of a group. If denied a model then, the more dependent members will become hostile in active (whining) or passive (withdrawal) manners. The more independent members will begin voting for themselves as the most acceptable alternative leader, running overt or covert campaigns for the office. As political camps develop, the leader can point out the split and thereby re-establish his expertise and his model potential. But he will be seen as a model no matter what he does, for he is perceived as having the corner on authority and experience. The behavior the leader chooses to manifest at this time will inevitably fashion the mold of the model.

A conflict is inevitable at this point: the leader wishes to divest himself of authority so the group will learn how to handle itself, and the group participants wish to invest authority in the leader in order to submit to it and relinquish responsibility for what will happen (or, as is often suspected early in a group's life, what will *not* happen since no one seems willing to organize and plan). Authority, even in its most vague conception, is a strong determinate of attitudes, and in an almost childlike way the group participants demand that they have some.

The leader is desired as a protector. The people in the group borrow strength from him, seek permission and reinforcement from him, and ask him to absorb their feelings as he seems to absorb his own. They use him as a counselor, either by attending to his words or by noting subtle behavioral cue systems as they did when they were students and had to guess the "right" answer by watching the teacher's eyes and the tilt of her head, by discriminating the tones of her voice, and the like. Insofar as the leader is aware of these practices, he will deliberately confuse the group by responding either at random with what seem to be inappropriate behaviors or by following a cue system of his own which has to do with the feelings and appearances of the group, rather than the questions or issues on the floor. On one hand the participants are struggling with questions of organization and expectation, while on the other the leader is already struggling with feelings and attitudes of which the group is largely unaware. At this point the leader is outnumbered — he is the only one who does not appear to be concerned about structure — and in a sense he is an alien in the group, at least with reference to this particular issue. He has become the authority of the group in an anonymous way, for the group participants do not know who he is yet or what he is really up to, though they are willing to obey him even if they have to make up their own commands and attribute them to him. This attribution is a sort of super ego function. It is not uncommon in children as they begin to wander out from under the constant gaze of their parents to explore the world. Old constraints remain to haunt the "good conscience."

In different ways and for different reasons the leader is seen at once as a professional, a seducer, a gift-giver, a model, a director, and an unwilling organizer. All of this adds up to his being an alien in the group, an authority cloaked and inscrutable, an authority who is frustratingly difficult to obey since he issues no demands.

trust

To me, trust is what makes risk less risky and more possible. Having trust is being assured that one can rely on another, at least under certain conditions. Unconditional trust is rare, for very few people have the capacity to fulfill all conditions for reliability in all circumstances. We generally learn whom we can trust under specific circumstances. In a group situation the leader is usually trusted from the outset as a competent professional and as an experienced group-maker. This trust is largely of a desperate nature for it is produced by suspicion and anxiety. Undergoing a group confrontation for the first time is a threatening business because it is a new experience, because it brings fear of exposure, and because of the popular fantasies of eroticism in groups which plague so many imaginations. Suspicion and anxiety are roused to a high level and need to be allayed by some sort of commitment to something or someone. The leader is needed as a keeper of the group's safety; he is needed as a source of trust.

There is by now no doubt that needs influence perceptions. When we are deprived of something we need we search it out. In this case when we do not trust ourselves or the strangers in the group, or for that matter the group process itself, a high need for trust in something is aroused. Any potential source of trust becomes flagrantly apparent to the perceiver, and in a group that source is the leader. He becomes a trustee, not yet a person who also needs trust. He is at first perceived as a source only. This cannot help from setting the leader apart from the rest of the group. If he is using a nondirective approach to the group growth process, he will make himself appear as an unwilling source for need satisfaction in an effort to become inessential to the nourishment of the group's development. He wants to become unnecessary (the aim of a good teacher) and is thus unwilling from the start to let the group depend on him.

The leader's reluctance to function as a source for need satisfaction is sometimes interpreted as a secretive, manipulative "technique." When it is so perceived, a common group reaction is mild rebellion, a testing of what limits exist, and an oblique denunciation of confidence in the leader. The rebellion seldom goes far, however, and the leader begins to be treated as a spy—a reticent observer who is compiling a mental dossier on every participant. We tend to be suspicious of potential sources of trust for we have all had the experience of certain behaviors in school going on "the permanent record" via reports by our teachers and some of our more socially ambitious peers. Early in the life of a group, the leader is trusted as a professional (and this trust is tested by asking the leader in many ways to please perform as he is expected to), but also mistrusted as a spy who is collecting information but not sharing it.

The spy role is partly a product of the leader's timing of his responses. It is true that he has a lot to say about the way a group is forming, but it is also true that providing this information too early creates a dependence which is difficult to overcome later on. His timing of his responses is intended to foster the growth of the group for it keeps questions open, and with the questions, curiosity. Curiosity has a tension of its own and this tension moves a group to explore what in fact it is up to. The same effect of timing applies to almost any individual learning situation.

Now the leader is leading a double life within the group (as the group perceives him) and thus is not to be completely trusted. A consequence of this is that the participants band together in their common plight, namely, that the "psychologist" won't tell them what is going on or what he thinks of each of them although they know he is observing them. The leader is to a degree ostracized from the group, for while the participants are trying to be more honest with each other (a function of tension created by curiosity and uncertainty), the leader is perceived as being dishonest – or at least as refraining from honesty. The leader has become an alien in an added sense. He remains "outside" the group because he is still seen in part as a traditional leader – someone who is needed to lean on for authority-support but not allowed to lean himself – and he is also "outside" the group because he now seems to be refraining from honesty while the others are becoming quite involved with it.

risk

Risk as it applies here is most properly a function of exposure, of self-disclosure. The physical analogy of dying of overexposure to the elements or to the environment suggests that exposure of the emotions or feelings carries a threat of psychological or ego death. To march unguarded and unprotected among the elements (strangers, enemies, etc.) one needs courage and some confidence that survival or strengthening will result from the efforts made.

There are two facets to risk in a group. The first is risking to expose oneself, and the second is risking to expose another.

A group leader naturally accumulates experience at both kinds of risk-taking during the course of his work. The more he is exposed to such behaviors and the more he is involved with them himself, the less threatening they become to him. Being familiar with one's reactions in risky situations and having experienced the relief and often the joy of its results tend to make such risk-taking desirable, and therefore less risky in terms of ego protection. A successful experience with personal risk tends to strengthen the ego, which in turn makes ego less of an issue altogether.

There is no more interesting topic of conversation than oneself. The person who does not want to talk about himself is rare: either he has no interest in himself or he has explored himself sufficiently to reduce the need and the pressure to *get at* the exploration. The first of these possibilities is so uncommon that there is nothing much to say about it. The second is, however, very important for the membership potential of a group leader.

Trust and risk are related in a very close way: they seem

almost mutually dependent. It is difficult to risk anything unless you can trust to some degree, and it is difficult to develop any trust without risking something of yourself and coming out with more confidence than you began with. Assuming that when a group begins the participants have no reason to risk anything of themselves because they have no reason to trust anyone present (except the leader as a professional), the leader again finds himself in a position unique to the group. He has risked before. He has exposed himself and others in similar group situations.

These two facets of risk (exposing self and exposing another) reflect two distinctly different behaviors. Exposing oneself at the risk of rejection by others is perhaps the less threatening of the two sorts of risk. One reason for this is that *you* have the privilege of choosing what *you* think *you* can deal with at any given time. The surprise aspect of exposure of self is reduced almost to insignificance. There is an anticipation process of working and warming up to a point where you are ready and anxious to reveal something, and this does not happen when some other tries to do the exposing for you. As confidence of acceptance by the group grows with experiences of risking personal exposure to a group, more and more of one's private doubts and questions become public and significant tensions are resolved. (See the section of Chapter 6 devoted to the Johari Window.) As these cathartic pressures are relieved, exposure or "acting out" needs dissipate and are replaced with certain comforts and assurances which lead to a desire to expose others so they can experience the same "settling growth." A desire to share comfort with others motivates prodding, encouragement, and sometimes goading which is often misunderstood as aggression. It is true that aggressive behaviors occur in groups, but trying to expose another is not always aggressive; it can be supportive and compassionate.

A group leader who has been through self-exposure many times is likely to feel that what he could say about himself again is rather repetitious and therefore to feel no immediate need to get into it. For the most part, group participants have not had this experience (which is why they are in a group in the first place), and they are frightened of it. As they find themselves exposing more and more of themselves to each other they will eventually come around to telling the leader that he has not said much about himself. He is again seen as an "outsider," this time in a nonrisking sense. As will become apparent later on, those who do not risk self-exposure in the group are the ones who have least chance of becoming full members of the group. To become a member one must be known by the group, and if one does not expose himself, one will not be known.

The second kind of risk-taking, exposing another, is what a leader spends most of his time promoting, though not necessarily by doing it himself. Whereas the first kind of risk has a relatively brief attraction for a group leader, thus making it progressively harder for him to get his membership in the group through it, the second kind remains a viable means for him no matter how long he works in groups. Each group is different, and encouraging exposure of others is always appropriate and never repetitious. The leader gradually gravitates to this exposure-of-another kind of risk while the participants are more naturally concerned with the first kind of risk, the personal exposure. In this way, the leader is separated from the group because he appears to have more courage in "getting at" the other members of the group. Each member senses this, prepares himself to meet the challenge with whatever armor he has available, and develops a sympathy with the other members.

Whenever one person exposes another and the exposure provokes deep feelings, the nonexposed participants rush to comfort the person whose feelings they have shared. Often this comforting takes the form of temporarily rejecting the person who provoked the response. As was suggested above, the leader is most generally the one rejected, either for doing the deed himself or for allowing it to be done. This situation always seems to resolve itself, mainly through a new strength the exposed person gains from the experience: it is often he who invites the rejected one (the exposer or leader) back into the group as a sort of thanks and as an extension of friendship. When this is perceived by the other participants, they realize the difference between a friendship born of a significant personal experience shared with some risk, and the kind of mere acquaintance with each other that they have had from the beginning. New pressures to participate in a meaningful and personal way are generated from a sort of envy of the friendship, which amounts to a desire to share a sense of personal meaning with others. I believe that literally every individual seeks and needs experiences with (intense) personal meaning. Such experiences are scarce among us information-oriented, busy people, and are all the more alluring for their rarity. When it becomes clear that one's present context is supportive of such experiences, one finds it difficult to give up the (another!) chance to share in them.

If the leader is perceived as directly involved in such a breakthrough, and he generally is so perceived, he gains a compatriot in his uniqueness within the group, and this is one of the first steps toward membership. Two people have shared something of themselves with each other.

acceptance

I view acceptance as personal and explicit, not as a general "love thy neighbor" feeling. In the discussion about submission to anonymous authority I might have included submission to gentility or to "just good manners" or to the most flaccid sense of Christian charity, which is an impersonal sort of deference. Genuine personal acceptance is based on knowledge and experience shared with the person who is accepted, and it may include the internal struggle we sometimes have in coming around to accepting someone who is not like ourselves. At this point, I'm willing to suggest that it is this *felt* acceptance originating from intimate experiences with another that is the basis of membership in a group.

membership

All four elements that develop in the context of group activity reduce the likelihood of the leader's being accepted in the same way as the rest of the participants. As long as he remains an authority of some sort, is only half trusted (i.e., remaining half-spy), and is perceived as a nonrisk taker (of the self-exposure type), the most he can hope to become in the group is an accepted leader.

My own experience in groups leads me to speculate that a leader may be accepted as a full member of the group only if he is first rejected, thrown out completely from the "group life" once that has been established. When the group feels or tells the leader that they can get along without him or that they would prefer to get along without him because of something he has done, then he is in the position of having to get permission for re-entry into the group. He no longer doles out permission, he *asks* for it himself. It is only when he is no longer *needed* that he can be sure that he is *wanted*. If being wanted is being accepted for what you are as a person, not as a leader, then being wanted is being a member.

It should be clear that being a member of a group is quite different from being a vital functionary within the group. It is different from being a teacher, trainer, guide, or counselor. These are all names of roles, not of any person. In the governing of the group the leader must be deposed from his seat as patriarch and elected to the house of commons, the group itself, which is the supreme governing body. No one else in the group has ever held the chair, so no other member has the same route to travel for getting into the group. In a sense, the leader has more to overcome than the other members of the group *because* he has been in other groups before.

Ordinarily the leader elicits faith from the participants— faith in his authority, in his knowledge, in his control—and this faith makes risking and trusting possible. But as long as others have faith in him in this manner, he is kept apart, for the object of faith is a source of strength, and a source of strength cannot be seen as weak (i.e., as one of the faithful) for then he would cease to be a source of strength. The leader must break this faith to gain acceptance as a full and equal member of the group.

In summary it might be said that unless a group becomes strong enough in its own life, in its own sense of itself, to dispense with its leader, the leader will not have a very good chance of becoming a member. And a sense of membership on the leader's part may be his most vital proof that he has indeed helped make a group.

a note on re-creational research

I have a rather uneasy (and familiar) feeling that any one part of what I have written above is vulnerable to the scrutiny of tough-minded researchers, but a distant voice reminds me that "all particulars become meaningless if we lose sight of the pattern which they jointly constitute" (Polanyi, 1958, p. 57). And it is the pattern that is important to me. This pattern is not a given in my view, but an elusive product of transaction between me and several similar contexts, an unintended product that emerged out of an experience. In Dewey's phrase, it is an event-in-context.

A research problem is suggested here. In following a research design to validate my hypothesis, I would first have to assume the hypothesis and then concentrate my observations on the effects all relevant actions, behavior, etc. had on the hypothesis. But by doing this I would be denying the unintended, emergent quality of the pattern. I would have an unspoken goal for the group and thereby I would be guilty of a manipulation that would alter the situation I meant to research. Instead of focusing on the actions of the group in their particularity, I would focus on the actions that seemed to lead toward or away from my hypothesis. The new situation may be researchable, but that is not my concern. Perhaps Polanyi (1958, Chap. 8) can help make my problem clear:

> . . . our attention can hold only one focus at a time and . . . it would hence be self-contradictory to be both subsidiarily and focally aware of the same particulars at the same time.

The pattern I have tried to describe I became aware of subsidiarily, and if I were to focus on it during the experience I would change it insofar as I am involved in the group from a different perspective or point of view. In reading this sentence, you are focusing on its *meaning,* and you are aware of each word, each bit of punctuation, only subsidarily. You do have the opportunity, however, to try it again, this time focusing on each word and ignoring the overall meaning. The experience of reading the sentence will be different for you and the meaning different as well because your new interest leads you to different things. The sentence itself is available for yet more readings; it stands there waiting for you, ready to be viewed in whatever way you want. A group of living people, though, are not a very reasonable parallel to a group of typed words. The people are affected and thereby changed by each "reading," by each experience, by each moment. One cannot read the *same* "human sentence" (group in relation) twice, and it is impossible for one of the words (individuals) in this sentence (group) to jump out of his place in it to read it without changing it.

In brief, the membership I have described cannot be the subject of customary psychological research. To know that membership has taken place, one must experience it—be an intimate part of it and not merely an observer. I agree with Polanyi's notion that there is a vital component of knowledge which is the (passionate) contribution of the person knowing what is known. This contribution is not opposed to "knowledge," nor is it an element to be overcome in "objectifying" what is known. The thing "known" that I have been trying to describe is essentially a feeling, a "had" feeling. I know I had this feeling, and I have tried to re-create in language an experience which was re-creational in itself—clear only after it had happened. I would suggest that this attempt is research, very like what Moustakas calls heuristic research (Moustakas, 1961).

This sort of research may be tough-minded in its own way. A reasonable starting point for doing such research well is the researcher himself. This beginning entails more than merely accepting the fact that at least one person is always present in research; it entails the introspective process of experiencing oneself as an instrument to the point where one can see and accept comprehension and compassion mingling. Traditionally we have separated these two elements or concepts of experience to refine and clarify each of them. Perhaps it is time to explore in research one implication of transaction theory, namely, that we reconsider the effects of our using pairs of distinct concepts (Thomas, 1968), especially those concerned with personal experiences.

a flea for your ear,
or
why most plans for humanizing education probably won't work

9

With so many fine minds and sensitive consciences fretting, experimenting, and driving themselves to find ways of creating a genuine cause for celebration in our struggle against ignorance and callousness in schools, it is difficult to understand why in fact we still can't celebrate much of anything. The reason couldn't be that no one cares, for many do care, and there is no apparent lack of inventive energy or capability to go along with this concern. Still we see sound ideas being developed into sophisticated systems and useful new materials only later to become (almost cunningly) neutralized in classrooms. They wilt.

In that process between a stated intention and the actual existential result, either something which should happen is not happening, or something that should not happen is happening. Too many good ideas turn out to be stupid, expensive, indifferent, or bad facts. I think this is a sad and wasteful situation, and I am determined to make some sense out of it.

The question that interests me is: What are we doing wrong in trying to get what we think or say we want? More specifically, I'm interested in those "wants" which are stated as goals of "humanization" or "individualization" in classrooms, because that's what I want, too (though the words themselves have become irritating to me as they are unintentionally satiric, and, as is so often the case, the words have, by many people, been substituted for the action).

The perspective I want to apply to this question is basically one of experiential valuation, which is just one way of determining what is important for you (ends) and how to proceed (means) on the determination. What I have in mind makes more sense (to me at least) in relation to an example, so the example will come before getting further into the perspective.

the ear

Most of the projects now being designed and tested in education are related to one or more of the following general interests: individualizing instruction, becoming a facilitator of learning instead of a teacher, and using a computer for something. Each of these interests takes many different forms. We find them talked about almost everywhere — in the office of the educational consultant who is trying to sell open-space concepts for school facilities planning, in the companies that are trying to sell flexible scheduling or programmed textbooks, in the teachers' lounge, counsellor's office, principal's office, board meetings, tea rooms, and beer halls – almost everywhere frequented by school people except classrooms. In most of the planning that is going on we are likely to hear at least one of these ideas mentioned, pledged, and exalted. Often the three are considered a single unit, a trinity, and are spoken of (by the strictly orthodox) as distinct but operationally inseparable. No matter what the project, we have little trouble finding a stated end-in-view that reads like PLAN's (Program for Learning in Accordance with Needs, developed by Westinghouse Learning Corporation and the American Institutes for Research; from Shanner, n.d., pp. 5-6):

> One of the major purposes of the computer-managed program of individualized instruction is to free the teacher from non-instructional activities in the classroom to relate to youngsters in an instructional way. Thus the teacher's task in the classroom is to facilitate learning.

This part of the statement is vague, but it is in vogue. The teacher's task is to "facilitate learning" in a program of "individualized instruction." Shanner (p. 6) goes on to say that the computer's role

> is that of monitoring and operating an informational system which is used as backup support so that the teacher can maximize the amount of time spent relating directly to the youngsters. . . .

This is the educational aim of the entire system, namely, to make use of a computerized information pump in order to free more time for the teacher to *relate directly with the students*. This is the end-in-view. The means to this end seems to be the computer-managed information system. Electric clerk work.

The intention seems to me desirable, timely, and admirable. An interest in making it more likely that teachers will relate directly with students is an interest I share. It is encouraging to see large corporations taking such an interest, for with the resources they have behind them, perhaps they can actually accomplish something that teacher colleges and universities have not been able to with their "paper routes." It is curious, though, that the stated intention of this project is not explained or justified; it is merely given as an obviously good thing to intend. Who would quarrel? The means, on the other hand, is described and explained at some length, which leads me to suspect that the people running this project (and many others like them) know a good deal more about machinery and circuitry than they do about the consequences of their use. H. G. Wells said science is the mind of our culture; maybe he was right. It seems that no matter what the goal or problem, there is always someone willing and bidding to use some form of computer technology on it.

At this point you could substitute your own example, such as computer *assisted* instruction, flexible scheduling, educational TV, language labs, micro-teaching, or any number of other modern conveniences designed to be used so that teachers will have time to relate directly with students. Just find what the inventor, researcher, or salesman says the thing is for, and then look at how it is supposed to work.

It is likely you will find that an enormous amount of resources, skills, and effort have been applied to the refinement and perfection of the means (usually a machine/system combination). The people who conceive of and manage these projects don't just sit around assuming what the means will be; they are usually highly skilled professional technicians who get and spend fantastic amounts of money to make sure the electrical impulses get routed properly throughout the system. The results of this sort of dedication are remarkable, and one day we may reach the goal of absolute efficiency in moronic (taken one by one, the functions of a computer are moronic) calculation.

It is also likely that you will find behind this dedication a statement to the effect that given the improvement in efficiency the teacher will now be able to relate directly with students. Because the teacher will presumably have more "free" time, he will presumably use it in an intelligent and compassionate way, namely, relating directly with students.

the flea

From the perspective of valuation mentioned earlier, I'd like to ferret out the assumptions in this example. These assumptions will eventually act to reduce the enormous efforts of many people to another mediocre memento of well-organized failure.

An end-in-view follows a desire of some sort. The desire follows a perception, or feeling if you like, that something is wrong with an existing situation. If nothing were wrong, if everything in the situation were fine, what would be the reason for desiring something different? Desire by itself, however, could take the form of benign fantasy, diffusive evasion, or, perhaps most bizarre of all, resigned repetition. These forms are hardly desired ends for they don't change anything, and in an offhand way they serve to maintain the existing circumstances. When a desire is connected with the resolution of an existing difficulty, impediment, lack, or conflict, then the idea of an end-in-view begins to form.

The thing that distinguishes an end-in-view from simple wishing is responsible consideration of the means by which the end may be accomplished. As Dewey has so often said, something cannot be anticipated as an end without considering the conditions necessary for its existence. Establishing those conditions is the operative description of means. Now just as the thing to be changed, improved, or resolved existed in a set of conditions, so will the new end. Insofar as the new end will be affected by the new conditions, the means to that end (the establishing of the conditions for its existence) will affect the end itself. In fact, the means will become part of the end, and the end may be considered a near last phase of the means.

If we can assume for a moment that this new end now exists, and that because it is a new situation it brings new insights, problems, or desires, the intimate connection between ends and means might become clearer. The new end is now a condition that gives rise to new ruminations, inclinations, and plans, which in turn become ends-in-view. Thereby the existing end becomes a means to further ends. The process of dealing with things that aren't just right, a process which involves desire and an end-in-view, is a continuous, reciprocal process.

There are two important implications suggested by this view. The first is related to the multiplicity of possible consequences which may follow any specific action. If we want this particular thing to happen (select an end), and we want to make it happen by this means instead of that (select a means), unhappily there is no guarantee that this means will lead to that and only that end. We simply can't control everything, anticipate everything, or even perceive everything. When we select an end, we are really only picking out a favorite aspect of what *might* happen. We have to be willing at some point in the process of creating the conditions for our chosen anticipation to revaluate the process in terms of other consequences which occur. So-called side effects – unintended consequences – are just as real for being unintended, and they must be considered in the process of reaching the favored end-in-view. They can be disastrous. Consider for instance the combination of an internal combustion engine and leaded gasoline (which keeps the engine knock-free, but through pollution knocks the hell out of the driver's insides). Thalidomide. IQ tests.

The second implication involves one's commitment to a selected means. Selecting a means is as much an act of valuation as is selecting an end. You are unavoidably assigning values whenever you make a choice. When there are alternatives (that is, when choice is possible) and you select one, you simultaneously reject the others. If the selected means turns out to have either too much effect (distortion) or too little (ineffectiveness) on establishing conditions for the existence of the end-in-view, a new problem must be faced. Modify or discard the means or the end or both. Obviously at different times, each of the three will have its turn. In this situation, however, I am by no means willing to discard the end, namely *teachers relating directly with students*, but I am afraid that if the end remains out of reach in the PLAN system described above, then directly or indirectly the people who are supposed to be served by the system will be accused of being inferior to it. My fear of an unassailable commitment to the technology in this system and similar projects is based on the dehumanized conditions and attitudes which already exist in schools, the very things we are trying to overcome. We continue to have too much reverence for the objects designed to help us and too little respect for the persons who need our help.

applying the flea to the ear

If we believe PLAN's stated end-in-view, then we might infer that the problem is to provide conditions which do not presently exist, wherein a teacher will relate directly with students. There are two parts to the solution of this problem: (1) to provide more "free" time, and (2) to insure that this "free" time will be used in a specific manner: in direct personal relations between teacher and student. If ends and means are in fact closely related with one another and if there is a reciprocal aspect to their functions and values, then we might expect that the "humanistic" character of the stated end would be represented and exercised in the means for achieving it. Otherwise, we would have to contend with a flagrant and potentially fatal contradiction: acting in the manner which the action is supposed to eliminate.

Assuming that the information system is what it purports to be and does in fact liberate previously captured time by assuming the routine clerical duties of scoring examinations (which is a dubious enterprise in the first place) and the like, the first part of the solution becomes a condition for the second part.

And that is where the system stops. And that's why it will fail. And that's why all the other "humanistic" educational projects which are represented by this example will fail. The second part of the solution to the problem, the designated use of free time, is stranded in a statement, an assumption that if there is time for it people will relate directly, personally, and honestly with each other. Learning how to use in-system time is one thing, but learning how to use out-of-system time is quite another, which nobody pays any attention to at all.

On what grounds can we justify the assumption that a teacher who has undergone mandatory training in certain "teaching behavior" will, at the drop of a printout, simply begin acting differently? Relating directly with people personally, intelligently, and compassionately is an *accomplishment,* especially within an institution which habitually punishes such behavior (lack of discipline, you know; doesn't *command* respect). There are no grounds for the assumption, and there is ample evidence to the contrary.

One of the many consequences produced by the "free time machines" was understood long ago by Parkinson: people are likely to take longer to do the same things. (No matter how far ahead a deadline is set, I always meet it. Exactly to the last hour.)

It is incredible that after the spending of millions of dollars to create one of the conditions necessary for the stated end of this project, the actual existence of the end is left to chance. Simple naive old chance. The whole system development was predicated on a concern about the burden of "things" which deform personal contact with persons into personal (in a loose sense of the term) contact with the things themselves. The response to this concern was to produce another thing – slicker, quicker, and cleaner to be sure, but still a thing – and then withdraw.

What should be done to salvage this and other such projects is to pay some attention to the people. Adults say that it is a good idea to individualize, humanize, and personalize the classroom. That means the people in the classroom would have a chance to relate to one another as directly, openly, and honestly as they can and choose to. If that's a good idea for the students, is it also a good idea for the adults: teachers with teachers, teachers with administrators, administrators with administrators, administrators with the board and public? That is a commonly wished-for yet challenging proposition. For many it is still in the wishing stage, and not yet an end-in-view because the conditions for its existence are not being seriously considered along with the desire. There is simply no way to mandate direct, open, honest communication between people. That's like ordering someone to be happy. It won't happen. It's stupid. It's as stupid as expecting a teacher to change his practiced conduct as a teacher because you have rearranged a time structure that was artificial in the first place.

I don't think the problem is one of time. All the time there is belongs to you, and you may give it away or sell it for whatever price, but it is yours to give or sell. I think the problem is fear. Fear that others don't feel the same as we do about sharing our time. The irony is that the "we" actually is a huge number of persons and the "they" is very small. We just don't believe it.

If you hold an end-in-view such as participating in direct personal relations with others where you can learn and help others learn, and if you believe that ends and means are intimately connected and mutually determining, then what is the most reasonable way to accomplish the end? The way I would suggest is to gather a small number of people who share the end-in-view and begin to help each other discover why it is that communications among you are not up to the standards of clarity and directness that you have set or that you desire. Try to relate with the others as directly as you can, and listen to the reactions of the others when you succeed and when you fail. You will find, I think, that there is no "end" to this process beyond trying to maintain the process itself. You will also find that in a surprisingly short time the quality of your relations with others will change appreciably. The ends (where you want to be) and the means (where you are and what you are doing) continually refine each other in the process of clarifying the relations *you are experiencing.* This is what I would call personalized learning, or humanized education.

The circumstances for this kind of experience may be facilitated by a system which frees time for it and by a person who is already experienced in small group communication and by an administrator who is willing to risk censure for encouraging (and participating in) direct personal relations experiences, but there is no way to do without the experience if relating directly with other persons is in fact the end-in-view.

The final question is, as my friend Don De Lay so delicately puts it: Are we willing to risk our human ends?

preliminaries
of a
learning theory

Co-authored by DONALD H. DE LAY

10

In the fourteenth century, before books became an available public commodity, scholars stood before large crowds of students reading from manuscript scrolls. The students were expected to memorize what they heard. In the twentieth century we have available not only all the books that we could possibly read in a lifetime, but an incredibly rich resource of other media and travel opportunities as well; yet our teachers still stand in front of large crowds of students and read from scrolls (albeit somewhat more up to date). The students are still expected to memorize what they hear. In six hundred years there have been a few relatively brief flurries of concern about how people learn, but the basic and ancient model of lecture-memorize-test is still, incredibly enough, accepted as *the* way.

Classrooms are so far out of step with what is going on in

the world outside (a discrepancy with which every student and teacher is familiar) that they have virtually become halls for an habitual conformity game. A child learns from his elders to play the school game in order to dissipate fear – fear of parent and teacher reprisal, of peer ridicule, of some sort of abstract failure to keep within the horizontal blue lines and the vertical red line margins, and, most sad of all, fear of making a mistake (which is to say, in many cases, being inventive). The fear comes largely from the same reprehensible adult behavior that provoked Alfred Adler to define education as "the process of transferring the notes of the teacher to the notebook of the pupil without passing through the head of either." He was joined in his outrage by Albert Einstein, who quipped that "Education is *what's left* when you have forgotten everything you learned in school."

It would be frighteningly easy to go on deriding the traditions of institutionalized education in this country, but the more important task is formulating a sound basis for improving learning opportunities. We cannot improve education without changing it, and we are reluctant to begin because changing always involves a risk. However, in light of the state of education now, a refusal to risk change seems a gross irresponsibility, for it means perpetuating a severe and general failure. Six hundred years is enough time for caution.

Our essential concern is for human beings. The assumption underlying the presentation of this theory is that schools abound with good people who really want to do a better job of helping students, who really care about their work, and who are willing to spend the vast amount of energy necessary for breaking through into improvement. If this were not true, we would have no reason for hope at all.

bases for learning

Hundreds of statements have been made about what the purpose of school is; to us, the best one is simply *to help students want to learn*. What we mean by learning is a change in personal behavior of which the person is aware. It may seem redundant if not naive to say this, yet many schools operate as if learning were a function of information accumulation alone. Learning, in our opinion, is a product of two functions: acquiring information and, more important, discovering and developing *personal meaning*. It is the combination of information plus its personal meaning to the learner that creates a behavioral change.

Learning = Information + *Personal Meaning* → Behavioral Change

Too often formal learning is artificially terminated by tests at the informational level. The behavioral change resulting from preparation for such tests comes in the form of finger movements on a test paper. Any first year algebra student can tell you how fast this imprint of "learning" fades and how significant it remains to him.

If we are serious about improving schools, we must look carefully at what we believe about learning, for we cannot make a solid case for change on any other basis. For the most part, learning is a unique, lonesome, personal process, even in a crowded classroom. The number of variances that exist in one human being, let alone among a group of people, is fantastic. These variances in multiple combinations account for differences in the ways people learn. It follows that if we want to be as effective as we can in facilitating learning, we cannot afford to ignore individual differences. To "individualize instruction" is a valid and desirable goal. What is astonishing, however, is the frequency of its verbalization contrasted with the paucity of its practice. We seem to find comfort in talking about better things, good things, even though we haven't the courage to do them.

Just as we tend to fear the unknown, change of any sort, we also tend to avoid personal matters in education. Yet learning is a personal matter. We must push ourselves to find ways of dealing with the ambiguous and of overcoming our fear of approaching people on a personal, individual level – the level at which we find personal meaning.

One obstacle to change is the traditional ethos or context of assumptions in which learning takes place. Currently most schools are fashioned after military or penal models which are basically control-oriented. The prime assumption is that persons within the confines of the institution need control because they are untrustworthy. This attitude is surely not conducive to inventive, risky, highly personalized behavior, which is to say, learning. For personal learning to take place in a school, the institution must be operated in such a way as to encourage teachers and students to act on the belief that learning and independence are more important than control. If this action is not permitted by the administration, any attempts to improve learning will be crushed into insignificance. Personal meaning cannot flourish in a tightly controlled, mistrustful context which does not allow for ambiguity and surprise.

student choice   This basis for learning is easily abused. There is nothing more restrictive for a learner than to be given alternatives of only token dimensions (for example, between A and a), or to be given no choice at all. It is important that a teacher provide as broad an array of alternatives as practicable at every juncture of learning for every student. This requires a lot of work. It is important, however, so that the learner feels correctly that he has the *right* to select what he *wants* to learn. One of the teacher's jobs is to inform the student of what probable consequences he will face once he begins acting on his choice. In this way the student takes responsibility (or at least shares it with the teacher) for what he does, for what he wants to do. This is a much different form of behavior than following rules and assignments against one's wishes. Alternatives are important, but student selection is vital for allowing learning to become a personal process.

active involvement   It is not what we put into a student through his auditory canals but what he displays through various behaviors that makes the difference in learning. To require a student to sit passively absorbing (or ignoring) teacher-talk is to encourage all forms of passive, nonproductive, sedentary behavior. Learning is essentially an active process, a *behavior* change. The behavior change may take many different forms, but insofar as the change is a consequence of learning (as we use the term), the new behavior will tend to indicate that an integration is taking place between a personal sense of meaning and action. It will be apparent that a connection is forming between character and conduct, belief and behavior, integrity and individuality. In other words, the learner will show that he knows what he is doing and that he feels responsible for his behavior. Sitting quietly and listening dutifully is passive and therefore a deterrent to learning as we have defined it. Personal meaning cannot evolve when a person is not involved in what is going on around him. It is difficult to be involved when not allowed to be active; without involvement choice is irrelevant. The only thing you can get out of a sponge is what you allow it to soak up, and you generally have to squeeze pretty hard to get back what you already had. The sponge, by the way, is left empty again.

One of the fundamental skills that we want students to have is verbal dexterity—the ability to handle thoughts in terms of words. We want them to learn how to talk. Why then are teacher talking and student quietude the core elements of teaching? Why do we expect a student to learn how to talk when we are forever telling him to be quiet? Most teacher talk is lecturing that has a negative effect on learning. It prevents active involvement on the part of the learner.

inquiry   The power for learning resides in keeping questions open. A rhetoric of conclusions presented in rapid-fire style does not provoke inquiring behavior in students. Instead it deadens curiosity. We should encourage curiosity in learners by raising questions, not by repeating conclusions, for it is in the search for answers (or further questions) by the learner that learning takes place. Learning is an *inquiring process*. We cannot present all pertinent knowledge or information to students—there is too much of it and it changes too rapidly. But we can help equip students with the necessary tools for inquiry so they may learn to deal with change per se and so they may search out their own meanings in terms of their own interests.

intrinsic reward   Perhaps the most talked about issue in learning today is reinforcement or reward. Educators are inundated with a mass of commercially prepared material that is based on the notion that information properly defined, segmented, and sequenced (programmed) can be "learned" more efficiently. The principal idea behind this kind of programmed material is *immediate* reinforcement, that is, the learner is reinforced after each frame or segment of the program. This reinforcement or reward can be anything from a "correct" to a smile to a jellybean, and the process seems to be equally effective with pigeons or people (although pigeons do prefer corn). When properly used, this reinforcement schedule is a powerful adjunct to learning. Most often, however, it is directed at informational levels and seldom does it have any relation to meaning of a personal sort. It seems to us that this issue could stand a revaluation; teachers have better things to do than act as reinforcement agents with their pockets full of jellybeans or with their faces set to smile.

The main trouble with this type of reward system is that the learner perceives it as extrinsic to himself, in the same way that he perceives the most common reward system used in education, namely, grades. Extrinsically perceived rewards tend to separate and barricade the learner from the subject and from the person directing the process and issuing the rewards. This may explain, in part, the need for *control* of students in most schools. It is ironic that the most common rewards given by educators drive students away from learning.

Sometime ago one of the authors (Don De Lay) devised a plan (CRAM: Comprehensive Random Achievement Monitor) to monitor student progress on a continuous basis through the duration of a course (De Lay and Nyberg, 1970). The idea was to give a rather short test in several different forms which represented a sample of the entire subject of the course several times during the semester. The questions were randomly selected from a master list of course objectives. By sampling responses to the material by different students at random intervals, he was able to monitor the progress of each student and the entire class. The tests were never announced ahead of time, and the questions sometimes were new and sometimes were repeated because of the way they were selected. The initial student response to this infringement of the rules of the game was silent and vocal disapproval, and in some cases real anger. For several weeks hostility was evident but gradually subsiding. The tests were always returned and never graded; the only marks were small checks on items the student seemed confused about. As the course progressed students began to realize that they were not being evaluated. Instead, the test procedure let them know how they were progressing, where they were weak, and what they already knew, and it gave them some idea of what they might like to pursue next. *Students began to request the test rather than object to it.* Their perceptions of the same test given under the same conditions were reversed from "an extrinsic evaluation" to "an intrinsic feedback" – or knowledge leading toward the learner's own goals. We think Carl Rogers was right in saying that "evaluation destroys communication"; when evaluation was eliminated, communication improved between the teacher and the students and among the students themselves. We are certain that personal communication is intimately related to learning.

When a student feels he is being *assisted* by knowing his own progress toward his own goals, he soon assumes an attitude of wanting to know and enjoying the process of inquiry. Feedback can lead to the joy of learning for its own sake, which in turn leads to the teacher's ultimate goal: to become unnecessary. Learning is a lifelong process. To become a "learning person," a student must consciously pursue learning and be comfortable in an indeterminate, ever-changing, exciting world.

In our efforts to be efficient with student feedback, we run the danger of losing the important human element of *concern*. We have never met a human being who did not respond to what he perceived as authentic, spontaneous concern about his progress or well-being from another person. This authentic human warmth of real concern transposes feedback from something that is merely important to something that is really powerful. It is vital that teachers lower their "stranger level" with students and risk really knowing students as persons. Concern is the heart of the process of human feedback, the force that raises learning to a personalized level. The ultimate loss in teaching is to insulate oneself from students by abstracting them into objects, for every student knows that he really exists right in the "here and now," and that his is a very personal, concrete existence.

respect   A great deal of evidence supports the notion that the way a teacher feels about his students and the way each student feels about himself are of critical importance for learning. When a teacher expects a student's achievement level to be high, the student's achievement level tends to be high. When a student is convinced that he *can* learn and that another (the teacher) also is convinced that he can learn, he in fact does learn. Conversely, when neither teacher nor student is confident that a task can be done well, the task probably will not be done well (Rosenthal and Jacobson, 1968).

It is extremely important that teachers believe in each student and that this belief be open enough to be perceived by the student. The expectations of the teacher and of the student tend to be fulfilled. In brief, positive self-respect is a requisite for learning.

all together   Student choice, active involvement, inquiry, intrinsic reward, and respect have been considered one by one as bases for learning. The learning process exists, however, as a complete experience with all its parts in motion, flowing as part of the living person. We have tried to establish the rudiments of a learning theory that acknowledges the flow and individuality of learning. Our theory points to the absence of any cure-alls for education, either in technical systems or structures of thought, including our own. If the freedom and concern that are essential to learning can come alive only in the context of a particular group of people, with all their limitations, then much of our theory may be wrong for that group. Freedom extends to the choice of theories, and we can only hope that each teacher would commit himself to some position in learning he believes in and then do something about it. As he shifts from an intellectual commitment to a behavioral commitment as well, *experiencing* the consequences of his ideas with other persons, then the refinement process of experiential learning can begin.

the theory in a school setting

Our illusive, indeterminate, personal, changing position in learning is impossible to reduce to a concrete model. The best we can do is to offer some examples of how the theory might work out in learning situations.

The whole process begins with a respect for individual differences, both in students and in teachers. The two main differences we are concerned with are interest and rate of progress. If we want to allow a student to act on his interests at his own pace, the teacher has a responsibility to present an environment which provides reasonable choices for each student. That is to say, quite soon in a course the teacher should present a wide range of material he would like to deal with, encouraging the students to decide how they want to get into it. This material *must* be a product of the teacher's own interests and feelings of competence. This is important because the feelings a teacher has about what he is doing transfer along with information: if the teacher is enthusiastic, the students are more likely to become enthusiastic. It is difficult to fool students by feigning enthusiasm; therefore, a teacher should teach what he *wants* to teach. Anything that jeopardizes students' interest in learning is a travesty. A bored teacher or a hypocritical one is a travesty.

With interest and enthusiasm comes involvement, and some sense of intimacy besides. How these elements develop and merge is a personal matter. A teacher cannot expect all students to follow his preferred involvement pattern. Rather he must allow divergent patterns to emerge. This indeterminacy is easier to bear when he is essentially at home with what he is doing, and the indeterminacy is *essential* if choice is to be allowed. Once the teacher is freed from imposing a predetermined curriculum of information, once he is teaching what he feels comfortable with, he will be able to engage the personal interests of his students.

One way to handle informational concerns is through the large group instruction mode which allows hundreds of students to share one teacher at his best. In this instance, all students taking a certain class (say English III) can be scheduled to hear a lecture on Keats by the faculty member whose special interest is Keats. The idea is to present a limited amount of material with high impact, and this can best be done by someone who has a high level of interest in the material. The lecturer should not provide answers or "cover" a unit, but should raise questions and encourage inquiry. Large group presentations do not represent learning directly; it is only in the students' use of the ideas and information presented that learning occurs. However, large group presentations can be helpful in starting individual learning.

It is important to remember that the key difference between large group instruction and small group instruction is not the number of students present, but what happens to them. A teacher can "present" to 500 students or to one student: it is always large group instruction if the teacher dominates the presentation. Teachers must be careful of subconscious or habitual dominance, and they must be vigilant in remaining open so that students may develop in their own personal ways.

Personal meaning can best be explored through small group processes. The opportunities for doing this in public schools are limited by class size and academic traditions, but let us examine the best possible situation. In this situation ten to fifteen students meet with their teacher in an atmosphere which must be *established* in the open as nonevaluative, free-flowing, and self-governing. Only in these circumstances will the membership phenomenon occur. This phenomenon is not mysterious or mystical; it is, rather, a normal consequence of extended face-to-face contact between students. (The phenomenon can be difficult for the teacher, as suggested in Chapter 8.) It indicates strongly that, given the chance, people would rather talk with each other meaningfully and openly than peripherally and defensively. If circumstances are not threatening, communicative interaction will transcend formal information exchange to levels of personal meaning, mutual support, and sharing. At this juncture students and teacher cannot play games; they must be themselves. It is a valuable learning experience to present a meaningful idea of one's own to peers and to an adult who will respond in honest and often unpredictable ways.

A situation of trust and nonevaluation makes personal meaning possible to the extent that fear of self-expression is reduced. The phenomenon of group membership is an indicator of trust: as people begin to share their knowledge and feelings, stranger levels go way down and personal risk levels go way up until mutual support and concern are realized through mutual acceptance. As the membership phenomenon occurs, group life becomes increasingly open, free, and functional.

During group development, the sensitive teacher will recognize a great wealth of data to aid his efforts in personalizing his teaching ("learning assistance" is a more accurate phrase for what he does). An increasing number of secure and open teachers are finding the joy of really knowing their students through this experience, which enables them to perform at their highest levels of competence and concern.

If these levels are to be attained, the school atmosphere, or ethos, must be perceived by the students as open-autonomous;

that is, they must perceive their freedom and responsibility in pursuing goals that they can choose. In many schools the atmosphere is quite different, and the efforts of a solitary teacher may be difficult, painful, and moderately successful at best. At worst, they may cause the teacher to quit teaching. The risk is real. When a feeling of active learning permeates an entire school, though, the emergence of independent, productive learners is predictable.

The curriculum in such a school could be produced from the interaction between students and teachers, from the autonomous use of independent time, and from the scope and range of personal interests. There would be no forced connection between teacher presentation and student work, a connection that may give the appearance of expanding interests, but that cuts away the reality.

A further word about student independence is in order, for at any given time in any course any student will be somewhere between the two extremes of needing a great deal of personal help and needing to be left completely alone. People change constantly and rapidly. A teacher must be sensitive to changes in others if he is to respond helpfully.

In sum, students should be provided a changing and expanding range of choices from which to *select*. They should be made vividly aware that they have personal responsibility in learning, that their performance is valued, and that learning is an *active* process. A narrative of *inquiry* should be initiated and every effort given to keep this personal inquiry open — terminating functions must be minimized. Adults in a school should be concerned enough with students to keep each one personally aware of his progress toward his own goals in an atmosphere of *intrinsic reward*. Above all, the student should be afforded dignity; he must know that adults and peers believe in him so he may believe in himself and develop *self-respect*.

These are different and difficult roles for adults in a school. On the other hand, it seems feasible that the personal energy needed to personalize a school may be far less taxing and much more rewarding than the effort needed to control a school. For example, it may be possible to stop trying to motivate students by *doing something to them* and replace this function with attempts to merit their consent, something *they give*. Rather than control all students at all times, perhaps it is possible to control only the very few who prove they need it and *release* the vast majority of students who really intend to do what is necessary to learn. The traditional adult role in schools — *giving* to the student what the adult wants him to get and then *taking* back from the student what the adult wants to prove he got — may be reversed so the student *gives* what he wants to the teacher and *takes* what he wants from the teacher. If fear of grades, reprisal and the "permanent record" were eliminated, authentic mutual trust could become a prominent characteristic of the school atmosphere.

School presently is a game for most students. If the incentives for playing the game were removed and the potentials for freedom and concern were provided, then students would have good reason to give of themselves, to risk the unknown in learning, and to enjoy the whole process. We believe that the vast majority of adults in public education are willing to risk themselves to make this happen.

inadvertent learning,
or
the harmonics
of being human

11

It is impossible to produce the equivalent of a pure sound wave in human communication. Any source of sound must set up vibrations in the air; these vibrations, as they play off various features of the transmitting context and of the receiver, produce subvibrations, partials, or overtones of the fundamental. Pure sound plus subvibrations becomes harmonic sound.

By analogy it is possible to see a similar phenomenon in most human doings. The source of any message, the context in which the message travels, and the characteristics of the receiver of the message, all get together in *creating* the harmonics of the message itself. A kiss, for instance, means different things to me depending on who does the kissing, where it's done, what led up to it, where it might lead to, and which part of my body is involved.

Praise from a person I respect is altogether different from praise given by someone I don't respect. The same is true for criticism, orders, homework, money, phone calls, movie or book reviews, et cetera. When I watch or listen to a person doing something, the flash of an eye, a gesture, a tone of voice, or merely a stance relative to me or others will produce a "sense" of what is going on, a covert meaning that underlies what is happening overtly. Everyone who has been aware of that "sense" knows how powerful it is in terms of credibility, the final impression made in a given situation.

How a person does is always part of *what* a person does. The *how* is closely related to the feelings a person has about what he is doing and about the people he is doing it with or for. The *how* is a conversion of relevant feelings into behavior, and it is not unusual that other people will recognize them even when the person himself does not. We teach our feelings, in a broad sense of the term, inadvertently. And because "cognitive" learning cannot take place without some feeling response (no person is ever absolutely devoid of feeling, though he might mistake depression, calm, or boredom for a void), we can never be certain about what exactly we are teaching or what exactly is being learned if we are not aware of the feelings involved. There is a good chance that the intensity of the feelings influences the intensity of involvement in the learning. If a student perceives that the teacher doesn't give a damn about what he is teaching, or that the impression the teacher is trying to make is a put-on, the student's own involvement is likely to remain on the level of a put-on or an outright rejection.

We've all had the experience of learning something (for example, the multiplication tables or quadratic equations) and because of the *experience* of learning it, either loathing or loving the prospect of doing more of it. We learn, inadvertently, so much more than mere subject matter, and teachers are a tremendous influence by virtue of their inadvertent teaching.

In trying to figure out why we know so little about what constitutes "a good teacher," Ernest Hilgard says (1966, p. 3): "My guess is that (studies on effective teaching) fail . . . to understand the subtle differences made by kind of student, kind of teaching setting, and kind of long-range goals that are operative." He goes on to observe (p. 9) that "reports of great teachers commonly stress their personalities, rather than their scholarship or technical teaching skills," and (p. 10) that there is some suggestion that what students get from teachers is "*caught* rather than *taught*."

An example of "catching" is given in the Rosenthal and Jacobson study, *Pygmalion In the Classroom* (1968). The title was inspired by Liza's speech to Pickering in the last act of Shaw's *Pygmalion:*

> . . . You see, really and truly, apart from the things
> anyone can pick up (the dressing and the proper way
> of speaking, and so on), the difference between a lady
> and a flower girl is not how she behaves, but how
> she's treated. I shall always be a flower girl to
> Professor Higgins, because he always treats me as a
> flower girl, and always will; but I know I can be a lady
> to you, because you always treat me as a lady, and
> always will.

I do not propose to judge the adequacy of the data analysis, nor methodological or ethical questions of procedure in this study. All I want to do is point out an example of inadvertent learning. Rosenthal and Jacobson made a random list of names from the student population at a certain school. They gave this list to the teachers in the school, telling them that the list represented a group of children who showed "unusual potential for intellectual growth." They said they just thought the teachers would like to know, so they would be prepared. The investigators found after eight months that the teachers' expectations had led to an actual change in the childrens' intellectual performance, and actual increases in IQ scores. Inadvertently, the teachers "taught" the selected students that they were expected to do better than ever before, that they were good students, and that they deserved attention. The children "caught" the idea and did something about it.

If it works for some, why not more — why not all? If what a teacher thinks of his students influences what the students do, how can we account for the overwhelming number of kids who are having trouble even staying in school? What must their teachers think of them, really? Of course you can't fake your feelings and expectations about kids. They see through it and learn that you are a fake. And they learn to fake you back. Whatever you are is contagious (see Hilgard, 1966).

We produce vibrations all the time in all we do, whether we like it or not, even when we are simply, "objectively" presenting a thing, a lesson. John Dewey says it well (1967, p. 47):

> There is no contact with things except through the medium of people. The things themselves are saturated with the particular values which are put into them, not only by what people say about them, but more by what they do about them, and the way they show they feel about them and with them.

There is no way to hide behind a curriculum or the status of "teacher"; to think so is folly, to try to do so is futile. What we learn, in school or out, depends more on the *experiences* we have than on what is intentionally taught. If we could learn to pay more attention to the experiences we undergo, share, and create together, we would probably stop worrying about mastering some teaching technique or another and become more aware of the inadvertent consequences of using "techniques" and "methods" on live people. Some of these consequences hurt.

For instance, I have talked with sincere, conscientious, hard-working young teachers who try daily to do their jobs properly. They try to teach as they have been taught to teach. And it bothers them that their students don't seem to respond with any interest and sometimes end up disliking them. They don't realize that they are creating the sort of context which leads, inevitably it seems, to a contest between "teacher" and "student." They don't seem to realize that a person's integrity is challenged when he is treated in terms of a generalized theory by a representative of that theory. In these circumstances a person knows that he is expected to respond in a predictable way, and he either must become an actor or try to discredit the theory and its representative.

The point is worth repeating. Standardized procedures are demeaning to individual persons. One consequence of "teaching the way teachers are taught to teach" is that students will be insulted and they will react with dislike toward the person who insults them or, worse yet, they will accept the treatment and deny their own integrity for the sake of taking such crap *cheerfully*. That is the most ignominious of all inadvertent learning.

As we voice our intentions of rearing or teaching children to be polite, well-behaved, loving, and lovable, I can't help remembering something that John Holt wrote (1964, pp. 167–8):

> . . . we like children who are a little afraid of us, docile, deferential children, though not, of course, if they are so obviously afraid that they threaten our image of ourselves as kind, lovable people whom there is no reason to fear. We find ideal the kind of "good" children who are just enough afraid of us to do everything we want, without making us feel that fear of us is what is making them do it.

We can create this situation simply by not being honest about ourselves with children, by presenting only the knowing, virtuous, strong, in-control-of-it-all, never-failing side of ourselves. We do this to give children someone to look up to, to rely on, to protect them, but we don't realize that children know they are not always that good, that strong, that right and the contrast, without ever being spoken, frightens them. It's a model that they *know* they can't live up to; therefore, they will *always* be liable to reprimand, punishment, failure, and a bad conscience. When a child is thinking this way, it's easy to see how lying and hiding and occasional attempts to bully or dominate make sense to him. Lying and hiding are for avoiding punishment; bullying and dominating are for showing some strength in an adult way. In all this the child will be imitating what he sees as a model. *And the model is ultimately based on fear and deception.* It is learned inadvertently, but thoroughly, by many.

We simply cannot avoid learning things inadvertently — things pleasant and unpleasant, actual and imagined, desirable and undesirable, simple and complex, helpful and hindering. The harmonics are there, or, as they say in communications theory, there is always "noise" in the system. I am not trying to suggest that we eliminate the inadvertent learning, for that would be impossible. What I am suggesting is that we take time often and regularly to check up on what it is and what effects it's having on what we set out to accomplish. The only way to check up on it is to ask the people around us what it is, whether and how we are coming across. And nobody is going to be willing to answer such questions unless we are willing to do the same for them. Knowing our inadvertent communications helps us to understand why we are not able to do what we want to do as well as we want to do it. It's a matter of clarifying relations among people so that stupid, wasteful, distasteful misunderstandings can be minimized. We have enough things to disagree about without needless misunderstandings.

The kind of talk I am suggesting here is out of the question for the devotedly insincere and for those incapable of trusting another person, neither of whom should be in education anyway. It's the kind of talk that has to be moved up on slowly, according to one's appetite, to get back in practice. It's the kind of talk that reminds us, as Dennison says (1969, p. 91),

> . . . the music of our ordinary conversations is of equal importance with the words. It is a kind of touching: our eyes "touch," our facial expressions play back and forth, tones answer tones. We experience the silences in a physical, structural way; they, too, are a species of contact. In short, the physical part of everyday speech is just as important as the "mental" . . .

It's the kind of talk that children use all the time, and we *must* get back in practice in order to share it with them, and with each other. It makes for a more tender world to live in, and a more living way of helping each other learn.

the same thing said less personally

Teacher training institutions emphasize the transmission of deliberate, intentional modes, means, and methods of instruction used in the transfer of information from one place (text, lesson plan, lecture notes) to another place (various memories). Learning is usually accounted for in terms of the quantitative success of such transfer. Very little attention is given to what I call inadvertent learning; that which is learned in spite of or independent of the deliberate instruction. As an example, a student will learn quickly what his teacher's attitudes are about the class, the subject area, other teachers, the school, and life in general. This is to say that *the teacher as a person is learned* inadvertently before or simultaneously with the information he is trying to teach deliberately. It is not unusual for a teacher to be blind to the fact that he is teaching himself as he is trying to teach some thing.

It is not difficult to overcome some of this blindness. He needs first to admit that what is true about how he sees his students is also true about the way they see him, namely, that they know more about him than he thinks they know, just as he knows more about them than they think he knows. Then, if both teacher and students share this "private" information they think they have about each other, they may accomplish much more with each other and probably enjoy each other more, too.

on
not beating up yourself
in order
to become a teacher

*If you stop visual fixing and imagining and pass
your palms slowly over your face without touching
it, you can suppose you are smoothing facial sur-
faces and you will be, since we tend to become as we
image and imagine.*

*This subject is taboo. No one investigates the finest
known instrument in universe, our own. We customarily overwork and overuse it, beat it up, wear it out
without ever once observing ourselves instru-
mentally.*

PAUL REPS, *Square Sun Square Moon*

12

It is startling, even astonishing, the ways we humans have of
establishing low estimates of ourselves and of arguing that
we should resign ourselves to them. Entire ideologies and the-

ories are bent on convincing us that we must accept what amounts to a politics of powerlessness, an impoverished human nature. It seems to me a serious mistake to take our humanity for granted. Our personal humanity, our future, is an *achievement,* not a given.

The classical mode of psychoanalysis is an example of a theory of low limits, conceptualized brilliantly into a very unbrilliant future. In brief, psychoanalysis holds that all behavior comes from a basically libidinal drive; that the limiting structure of personality is established by approximately age six; that the way to solve neurotic problems is through a re-examination of previously familiar things, people, and relationships — which is an orientation toward historic existence at the expense of the present and possibly the future; that the goal is adjustment to historical and social forces so that stability may be *maintained*; and that the analyst's value is couched in his impartiality and impersonality, a pose which deprives the "patient" of any chance to test his sense, his self, or his soul, as he is in the present, with the analyst as another human being. Thank goodness men like Burrow (1927), Rogers (1942, 1951), and Perls (1951) have seen the implications of this flagellantly deterministic view of personal humanity.

Psychoanalysis is only one of several reductionist theories that tend to turn us into little runts and that tempt us to beat ourselves up if we do not conform to the models provided for us. The philosophy of naturalism asserts that human values are derived from biological needs. Hedonism goes one step further with the idea that pleasure is the ultimate value. Neither of these views takes into account the higher qualities of discontent that we constantly nourish ourselves on and out of which genuine achievement is born (see Farson, 1969). Neither takes account of the world of symbols (without any necessary philosophical or theological implications) which is incomparable to the biological world. Our lives do in fact include symbols which refer to many things at once (a sign usually has only one referent); we cannot deny the connotative power of poetry or of a single good idea, nor can we deny that we resist rest and pleasure as ends. Rest and pleasure are only stopping places which provide further opportunity for activity and new interests which are also, in some respects, problems or dilemmas. Our being *involved*, actively a part of something, seems to be more important than the homeostatic ends of rest or pleasure. How many people do you know who are joyous over the prospect of sitting or sleeping for the rest of their lives?

The psychologies of environmentalism and stimulus-response behaviorism are similar in that persons are conceived as responding only to *outside* stimuli or at least similar in that such stimuli are the only ones that matter. Locke's *tabula rasa* model of the human mind is fundamental to both views (which leads me to wonder about the connection between the model of an erased tablet and the preponderance of chalk boards in classrooms – are the chalk boards really extensions of educators' views of children's minds, or of their own minds?). I sure as hell don't think of myself as a blank slate; if I did, I could not hope to do or feel anything that hadn't been done or felt before by someone else.

A final example of a reductionist view of us is the cyclical theory of history. According to this notion, history repeats itself, which means we repeat ourselves according to a grand design of failure: cities, cultures, and civilizations rise and fall inevitably. This means, in essence, it doesn't matter a whit what we do to make our little earthly nest a better one; there is no point in trying to educate anybody about the preferability of justice and brotherhood over tyranny and racism, for the latter are prophesied to rule us repeatedly, world without end. Amen.

It is precisely these kinds of advocations of powerlessness, these abject views of personal humanity, that lead to the cynical, possessive, philistine politics of our institutions. Educational institutions included. The wall that we are all up against is the poor estimate we have of ourselves.

authority and or respect

One favorite way some people have of beating up themselves is by deferring to others their right to make personal judgments. A personal judgment is an expression of conscience, a valuation. To defer such expression is to demean the worth of one's conscience. It makes a bruise on the tender insides; it makes a quiet injury where pain can in fact drive men mad.

Expressions of conscience almost always involve self-assertion – putting oneself forward – and self-assertion nearly always involves facing up to an authority. That's the hard part. We are taught to "respect authority"; however, we are not often taught that in matters of conscience *we are* the authority and we must learn to respect *ourselves*. Even if we allow someone else to represent us as an authority, we still *choose* to let him be our spokesman. We must remember that this choice is not irrevocable. When we forget this we are faced with the situation of choosing to stop making choices. Even worse than that, when we recognize that a previous choice turns out to be a bad one, one that comes in conflict with conscience, but we decide to go along with it anyway, we are actually *choosing* to do something we consider bad. Whenever "respect for authority" leads to doing things we consider bad, it's time to reconsider the respectability of that authority. There is no moral justification for allowing an authority, an agent to whom we have *given* authority, to make us act against our own conscience. The Nuremberg war trials even made it a crime to do so. A person who gives away his own conscience is nothing, even if he gets or keeps a good job, or even if he gains the whole world for that matter.

One of the things authorities and experts do is intimidate nonauthorities and nonexperts. Somehow we have gotten into the habit of ascribing almost magisterial rights and privileges to certain social positions, so that the occupants of these positions can assume an attitude of indignation when questioned or challenged. The implication of this attitude is that the questioner is somehow rude or inadequate, and that he is failing to recognize his place (see Chapter 7). The problem is that we have so much trained-in reverence for competitive achievement that we tend to mix it up with personal worth. We sucker ourselves into believing that we are less worthy, have fewer rights of opinion, and have lesser abilities in making decisions than someone who occupies another (usually referred to as "higher") social position, or who has a different set of certificates. That is an entirely different thing

tough and tender learning

than respecting another's clear thinking, insight, skill, or sincerity.

againsting and withing

Most teacher-training programs (and, for that matter, most preparatory courses that involve human relations) place great emphasis on theories and methods of instruction, learning, and conduct in general. This emphasis implies that a person should put aside his intuition, his contextually bred feelings, and his own personally responsive behavior in favor of one or another established rational models when he eventually gets down to dealing with people. The programs spend little if any time on nurturing intuition, recognition of feelings for what they are as they are felt, or flexibility and comfort in responding personally in different situations. In such programs the students are taught the discipline of againsting themselves, and presumably if they learn it well, they will pass it on to *their* students.

What is left out in this training is the real "inside stuff," the immense treasures to be found inside each living person. In our society we assume a split between "inside" and "outside," and we judge the two separately. At present the latter is *treated* as if it were the more valuable, while the former is *spoken of* as the more valuable. As Laing suggests (1967, p. 87):

We are socially conditioned to regard total immersion in outer space and time as normal and healthy. Immersion in inner space and time tends to be regarded as antisocial withdrawal, a deviation, invalid, patho- logical *per se,* in some sense discreditable.

At the same time we talk of peace of mind, integrity, a "clean" conscience, and the capacity to love and be loved as our high- est values. In fact, these things need and deserve our careful attention if they are to be clearly understood or fully realized in our behavior. It is peculiar that we do not pay more atten- tion to and exert more energy on developing the capacities and qualities that we say we value most in ourselves and in others. We would never leave the planning and building of a bridge from one shore to another entirely to chance or to one man alone. Why then do we leave the development of the per- sonal understanding that makes an effective and reliable bridge of human communication entirely to chance or to each man alone? The question is especially pertinent to the train- ing of teachers, for teaching *is* communication.

Most of the attempts made to structure techniques for communication between teacher and student are based on an old assumption about human minds. The assumption is that "mind" is a separate thing, a special isolated datum that functions discretely and is to be approached directly, as one would aim at a target. The philosophies which challenge this assumption are not popular among educators – it is difficult to find a school run on the bases of phenomonology, existen- tialism, experimentalism, or transactionalism. Without going into each of these positions, I would like to offer an analogy which will serve, I think, to make the essential point.

The analogy is taken from a statement in David Bohm's *Quantum Theory* (1958, p. 161):

> . . . at the quantum level of accuracy, an object does
> not have any "intrinsic" properties (for instance wave
> or particle) belonging to itself alone; instead it shares
> all its properties mutually and indivisibly with the
> systems with which it interacts.

In terms of quantum theory, the mind connot be approached directly, either to "instruct" it or to "measure" it, for it is not an "it" at all, but a characteristic of the immediate system in which it exists, namely a whole person. In making contact with another's "mind," a teacher makes contact with all the related properties of the person as well. If the teacher is ignorant of this, if he divorces himself from considerations of feeling, intuition, motives, attitudes, and all that is present in every living person, he is likely to botch the enterprise of trying to "instruct a mind."

Expanding the analogy one step further, every person shares properties with the systems with which he interacts. He has a mutual and indivisible share in the character and quality of any context he is in. If a teacher understands his function in a class this way, he is likely to discover some value in paying careful attention to the relations within the class, for he probably will discover more effective means of communicating with the other persons present. The elements of a system or context affect each other, sometimes in clearly visible ways, sometimes inadvertently. In order for the system or context to work smoothly and well, the elements of it must work with each other, not against each other.

From this point of view the relations among people and their interests, abilities, and attitudes take priority over any set curricula, timetable, or specific method of instruction.

This is because such relations and individual characteristics have within them the potential for determining the success or failure of any plan.

If important relations are misunderstood, then againsting is the game. If these relations are attended to and properly understood, then withing is the game and things begin to move. No matter how well a teacher imitates a model or how well he knows his subject matter, if he is againsting himself and againsting the important personal relations in the class context, he will drastically undermine his own potential to help others learn. If he tries to force a previously determined set of relations on an existing but yet unexplored context, he will either succeed by breaking the spirit of the students (while they are in his presence at least), or he will have to spend a disproportionate amount of time figuring ways to get students to pay attention to him and punishing them when they don't. Neither activity has the least to do with learning.

If we consider the person who is doing the teaching as much an influence on what is taught as is the "method of instruction" or the "curriculum," then the teacher would be wise to pay as much attention to the way he does things as to the things he does. Following the quantum analogy, the person, the method, the curriculum, and the learners constitute a whole. It simply does not make sense to ignore the personal parts, in which the energy of the whole lies, while trying to deal with the method and the subject. In other words, the persons in the classroom are as valid a subject for study as any curriculum topic.

The way of approaching the study of personal relations is really quite simple. As McGlashan (1967, p. 125) suggests:

> . . . it is possible for a human being in a period of
> relative personal security to give heed to those stim-
> uli which hitherto have been ignored.

All the teacher really needs is a period of relative personal security and some evidence that there is a chance of being
heard and understood if he and the students try to express
something that they care about. There is no special small
group technique that he has to learn to understand better the
personal relations that he is already in. All he has to do is
listen hard, make sure he understands what other persons are
trying to say by asking if he has it when he thinks he has it,
and respond as sincerely as he can to what others try to tell
him.

In an article on the "Characteristics of a Helping Relationship," Carl Rogers (1958) said:

> The point is that technique or theoretical orientation
> are not the force of fostered personal growth, but
> rather it is the manner of the therapist's (teacher's)
> *being* when at work.

Working hard at understanding and being sincere does not
imply that one must "bare one's soul" or force others to do so.
It does imply that a better understanding of distances and af-
finities among people can be achieved and *must* be achieved
if people are to work and simply be together in a more learn-
ingful, productive, and cooperative way. Although these goals
are stated by most teachers and most school districts, the
means I am suggesting to reach them are anathema to many.
From my experience of working with school people (teachers

and administrators), I would guess that one of the strong fears of small group communications is that organizational stability will be threatened, if not weakened and destroyed. This shows a clearly misanthropic view of one's colleagues, a view with which I strongly disagree. I have seen and experienced authority, with all its intimidative, fearful, mistrustful aspects, replaced with a sense of mutual respect which is much more stable than the authority had ever been. It is true that old structures of authority are weakened when people better understand them and the people in them, but the encouraging fact is that new systems of cooperation — based on a clearer view of the necessary personal relations in the system and on the respect which comes from an experience of mutual sincerity — evolve to improve the old structure. I have seen this happen in the administration of schools and in the operation of classrooms.

These experiences have strengthened my assumption that most people who work in schools are basically good people who want to do good work. All they need to do so is a situation that offers the personal security which comes of understanding the situation better: when they understand that most people in fact share a need or a desire to trust each other, it is far less threatening for them to act naturally.

None of this will make sense, of course, if you believe that acting naturally, having psychological liberty, will lead to meanness and destruction, rather than to compassion and creativity. Nor will it make sense if you don't believe that people everywhere, especially in a democratic society, have the *right* to share in the decisions which affect their lives.

Set teaching methods, curricula, and timetables are not the

only means by which we box ourselves in. We now have innumerable sets of packaged materials, computer-assisted and computer-monitored programs, flexible time-schedule printouts, and the like, which people are to deal with in prescribed methodical ways. This production of materials amounts to replacing an old set of things with a new set of things, which is quite different from encouraging individuals to respect their individuality and act naturally in using whatever things are around. To truly make learning an individual, involving, meaningful experience, we should pay more attention to individuals than to the specific things they have to play with. What happens in a classroom should come out of the relations and interests of the individuals involved, rather than out of some company's warehouse.

The teaching I admire is based on whole persons responding to whole persons, sharing interests, exploring unknown things, learning to trust one another, focusing on present personal relations, engaging in democratic decision-making, and taking responsibility for personal judgments. This kind of teaching cannot be done by a person who has a low estimate of himself or of his students. It cannot be done by a person who beats himself up in order to satisfy some authority, someone else's conception of what he should be like.

People desire affection, respect, and security. Most of us are even willing to lie for them. Then we get lies in return. *It is not necessary* to lie, to deny conscience, to hide. Somebody has to stop the lying and hiding in schools, and stop teaching lying and hiding to kids. Somebody has to take the trouble to examine his own self, his own style of life, so he can feel his personal humanity and can meet new situations on the merit of himself as a person rather than on the presumed merit of a credential or a course of training. To be an example of this is the best thing a teacher can do for kids: to make it possible to experience affection, respect, and security, and the exhilarating freedom of not having to lie, is the absolute, rock bottom, best goddamn thing any person can do for another. It opens the world.

on the possibilities
of being
a respectable teacher
without having
to push people around

It is no problem at all to locate jobs requiring an orientation toward achievement, competition, profit, and mobility, or even toward a higher standard of living. But it is difficult to find one requiring outstanding capacity for love, kindness, quietness, contentment, fun, frankness, and simplicity.

JULES HENRY, *Culture Against Man*

13

Discipline is a word for what teachers usually resort to when they are not making it with their students. When the teacher is being a bore and the students, not wishing to give their time entirely to boredom, create some diversion among themselves, the teacher becomes offended and summons his powers for punishment. That, incredibly enough, is like saying "If I'm boring, it's *their* own damn fault." At least the discipline break interrupts the monotony.

If a teacher were able to respond to the restlessness, impertinence, rudeness, or simply the noise that comes from disengagement by trying some other way of providing something to be thought about, talked about, or done, then the whole question of discipline would become irrelevant. The question of discipline would be displaced by questions about the fundamentally democratic processes of developing cooperative regulations, standards for social rights and courtesy, and necessary rules.

The type of class I'm talking about here would lie between the "authoritarian" type on one side, and the dread "permissive" type on the other. Herbert Kohl has made an interesting book under the title of *The Open Classroom,* in which he offers the following distinction (1969, p. 15): "'Annoying behavior' is legislated out of existence by the authoritarian teacher; pretended out of existence by the permissive teacher; and dealt with as a fact of existence by the open teacher."

In the authoritarian style, legislation does not affect the annoyance itself, only its expression, and that mostly for the teacher's satisfaction, not the students'. To the source of annoyance is added resentment. The pretense of the permissive style deals with neither the source nor the expression of annoying behavior. This sort of impersonal tolerance is insulting and frustrating; it is tantamount to partially denying the existence of a person, slicing part of him off, pretending part of him is invisible. It is also fraudulent (possibly Freudulent), deceitful, and disrespectful. The open style is an attempt to treat such things as annoyance with the same respect one has in treating other facts which are less unpleasant.

The essential character of an open classroom is a disposition toward encouraging frank consideration of all the situations that arise out of the live relations among all the persons present. It is not so much a program or model as it is a style, a way of approaching things. Sylvia Ashton-Warner, a brilliant renegade of a teacher, puts it this way (1965, p. 91):

> The only thing I step forward to teach is style. And
> believe me, I teach that. I teach it all the time in
> everything, because the rest follows. I teach style,
> and only style.

The thing to remember about openness and style is that they are not *things done* but *ways of doing* things. When the style is there, when the teacher can talk with students about their (and his) fears and confidences in an open way, then the subject is easier to perceive. The connection of style and subject is most evident in terms of comfort. Lack of comfort, which is commonplace in classrooms where disruptions are squelched or ignored, blocks learning. It is difficult to concentrate on a book when you have to go to the toilet. It is hard to work up enthusiasm about symbolism in English literature when you just missed getting hit by a car. It is almost impossible to get interested in a lecture if there has recently been a death in your family. There are certain things that have to be dealt with before other things can be dealt with at all adequately. One has to be comfortable in certain respects in order to concentrate.

When Ashton-Warner says she teaches style, I think she means particularly that she is always conscious of the importance of being genuine with her students and of encouraging genuine (as opposed to imitative) expression in others. "All else follows." Of course, to be genuine, sincere, and honest with others it is necessary to have some confidence in oneself and some trust in the others. These things, a sense of self-confidence and a sense of trust, add up to a positive feeling of comfort with others. When this kind of comfort is consistently pursued and gradually achieved, then learning is truly enriched. So much more can follow when a quality of being together is treated as a *priority* in a classroom. It makes the business of sharing information, experiences, and feelings, and of creating new experiences through which persons learn—that is to say, "teaching"—so much easier, more effective, and more enjoyable because everyone is involved in its doing.

From this point of view, the old principle about establishing control and discipline on the first day of school so as to avoid later complications and disorder must be replaced. That principle tends to justify itself. It exacerbates feelings of discomfort and distrust to the point of seething suspicion or lifeless resignation, which we all have seen expressed so inappropriately on young faces. I doubt if many people love that authoritarian kind of order, but most of us like and need a sense of clarity in our relations, that is, a natural order which comes of clarity.

The way to pursue this natural order, starting with the first day of school, is set about discovering each other's styles of learning by trying to establish a comfortable situation which will allow such styles to emerge. As the work of understanding each other progresses, the questions of rules and regulations, rights and courtesies, and appropriate procedures will come up. And because these questions come out of the class as a group, they can be dealt with by the group (I am assuming that the teacher is an active participant in the group). This seems to me a much more reasonable, desirable, and effective way to begin learning together than is the more traditional authoritarian way. It is also, in itself, a valuable lesson in democratic decision-making processes, a lesson which is usually taught ironically and paternalistically from an authoritarian position.

This suggestion implies that a teacher should experience work in small groups that focus on clarifying the styles and the relations of the participants during his teacher training. I think such experience is very important for people who are planning to influence the lives of other people by committing intentional acts of education. I think teachers have a serious moral obligation to aid a student's sense of worth and his ability to trust others, for the lack of these qualities makes all else either vapid or frightful. The only way to share these qualities, to introduce others to them, is to have them. The way to know you have them is to experience them with others, and that is what small group communication is all about. Small groups are not mysterious; their function is to replace with clarity the mysteries people wrap around themselves. But they are fascinating because, clearly seen, people are fascinating.

ambient adultomorphism

Adultomorphism is a strong tendency for interpreting a child's behavior in adult terms. It is to this malady that we owe most of the incredible variety of ways a child can "fail" at something. A child knows that he makes mistakes and blunders but they *become* other things to do, they change things around and point to new things, and they are just as intriguing (maybe more so) as straightaway accomplishments. Adults see activities from a success-failure view of things. A child lives more with an interesting-uninteresting view of things. Remember?

Sometimes it's hard to remember. "To a grown up person who is too absorbed in his own affairs to take an interest in children's affairs, children doubtless seem unreasonably engrossed in *their* own affairs" (Dewey, 1961, p. 44). A teacher who feels that he is not involved with some class activity sometimes thinks that no learning is taking place. Children do not need teachers as much or as constantly as adults want them to. It is important, however, for a teacher to pay attention to what children are doing so he can learn from it, even when he is not directly involved.

One of the things George Dennison (1969, pp. 210-11) noticed was that children, as they are relating to each other by means of some active enterprise, do not

> develop the specialized repertory based on the weak-
> nesses of others – as adult society abounds in special
> services, and those who specialize find themselves
> relating to, and untimately depending upon, the in-
> sufficiencies of others. Children relate to one another's
> strengths and abilities, since only these make
> enterprise possible.

What would a teacher do if he decided to stop leaning on the insufficiencies of his students? He might relate to them through active enterprises in which he sees to it that everyone gets a chance to exercise his strengths and abilities, confronting "insufficiencies" only when they become relevant to furthering the activity. This cooperative attitude would do much to reduce adultomorphic symptoms.

An interesting variation of adultomorphism was noted by Jonathan Kozol (1967, p. 57):

> . . . many teachers . . . make the mistake of attributing their own obtuseness or sense of isolation to the children they are teaching and that, having little faith in the communication of man to man themselves, they do not really believe you can get through to children either unless you spell everything out in these awful singsong terms.

Adults often feel they are doing a child a favor by reducing communications with him to a pappy patter, but they seldom realize that by doing so they are demonstrating that lifeless, dreary, condescending talk is what a child can expect if he hangs around adults. The language children use with each other is vivid, energetic, direct, engrossing, and unquestionably personal. The language a person uses makes an impression, and the impression of impersonal singsongery is not exactly encouraging. Why would a child want to talk with someone who gives him that impression? What's the attraction for him?

The point is that children have a strong interest in each other (which is seen by some teachers as an enemy of what they call teaching), and they might well show a strong natural interest in an adult teacher. But he cannot interest them by command or solely by virtue of being the teacher. He can interest them simply because he *is* interesting. I would venture to say that any teacher who is not putting up a sham, who has not adopted an impersonal, borrowed manner and language to use in class, would be interesting – because he is "real" – to a student. As Alan Watts puts it (1966, p. 130):

> The people we are tempted to call clods or boors are just those who seem to find nothing fascinating in being human; their humanity is incomplete, for it has never astonished them.

intensive waiting

In his book, *The Savage and Beautiful Country,* Alan Mc-Glashan (1967, p. 9) makes a point about the synthesis of thinking with feeling with the words of Simone Weil: ". . . silent, patient waiting for truth is an activity more intense than any searching." This thought is not to be confused with a call for passivity; alert waiting is an activity, though not the kind of activity commonly thought of. It's the activity of preparing to receive; it's being receptive in the sense the poet Keats meant in his description of "negative capability." It involves the assumption that something will come, that what is important will appear, if one can suspend for a time those expectations and anxious projections which are used as probers to hurry things up.

An example of this waiting is the experience of trying to recall a name and being unable to until, after you stop trying, it pops into your head. I have had similar experiences in the small groups I've worked with: I have nearly exhausted myself trying to decipher the meaning in the noise of a discussion until I just give up, sit back, and keep on paying attention *without trying to analyze* what I see and hear. I simply let it come into me. *Then* I begin to understand what's going on. It almost seems as though the face of clarity was turned away from me while I was poking it with my pointed reasons and contradictions, and then turned back to me when I put down my pokers.

I still have trouble remembering this lesson because, like so many others in our culture, I have developed some sort of reverence for efficiency. It is somehow vaguely *immoral* not to be anxious about time, not to be busy or trying hard. I know now from my own experience that in some cases, especially when other people or ideas are involved, it is *more* efficient to wait, to actively wait, than it is to chase and probe. But it doesn't *look* efficient. In other cases, such as sweeping the floor or rescuing an endangered princess, waiting doesn't help much. Also, for the teacher who is more interested in presenting all his material in a fixed time than in checking to see what or how anybody is learning, it doesn't make much sense either.

Kohl (1969, p. 20) found in his teaching that suspending expectations is an act of will and an approach to "objectivity." What he means by "objectivity" seems similar to what Edgar Friedenberg means (1965, p. 247), namely a capacity

> . . . to discern the properties of external reality without attributing to it the properties he would wish it to have, or believing himself to be responding to it when he is actually responding to his own needs and feelings.

Among the "external realities" are persons other than oneself. Being able to discern their characteristics, needs, feelings, thoughts, and the like is contingent upon being receptive to them as those persons show them. A racist cannot do this when race is an issue because he has certain immutable expectations and he responds to *these* instead of the persons who are the objects (literally) of his expectations. One could say the same of an avid IQist, trackist, or streamist.

James Herndon has expanded this general notion into a means for discovering how a class organizes itself, a phenomenon which occurs whether or not a teacher is aware of it. Obviously, it's better if a teacher is aware of it, and this is why Herndon thinks not many are (1968, p. 167):

> It's really almost impossible for adults, and no doubt especially for adult teachers, to see anything "constructive" going on in a bunch of kids shouting at each other. All the adults can see is just that: kids, all bunched together, yelling at each other. You can't believe they are doing it for anything you'd call a purpose; they are simply creating a problem, something that shouldn't exist at all.
>
> The adults also can't imagine that this problem is going to cease to exist unless they, the adults, make it cease. They feel that unless they issue orders and directions and threats, the kids will never stop making noise, never stop yelling, never get organized.
>
> This feeling is wrong. The adults are wrong on both counts, not because they are stupid, not even because they lack . . . "insight" either. They are wrong because almost no one can stand to wait around long enough without doing anything, so that they can see what all the shouting is about, or what might happen when it eventually is over. They can't stand to, and so they never find out. Never finding out, they assume that there was nothing there. I don't think the quality of insight is unique or even rare. . . . What does seem

to be rare is the ability to wait and see what is happening.

Any teacher who becomes embarrassed because of the noise his class makes, who is afraid of what some other adult will say about it, and therefore keeps things quiet, will probably never discover what is going on in his own room.

There are possibilities of being a respectable teacher without having to push people around. One can learn to participate in democratic decision-making processes instead of resorting to arbitrary discipline; one can learn the importance of personal style based on feeling comfortable around others; one can learn to recognize one's own adultomorphic symptoms; and one can learn to actively wait, to receive what the situation and other persons are offering.

why good conversation
is better
than any method

Being understanding, when one is able to do so, is
rewarding in its own right even though it is not the
same as feeling understood. But when it is mutual,
when you and I understand as well as feel understood
simultaneously, then for that moment the world is
home and bread is baking in the oven.

JOSEPH LUFT, *Of Human Interaction*

14

As the expressive candor of childhood is gradually restrained
by persistent social custom, what was a clearly understood
and respected part of every activity, clarity of personal regard,
becomes a question. The question is: What do people think of
me, how do they feel about me? And this question haunts
every one of us preemptively in literally every contact we
make with another person who has lost his candor. Every
lover, employee, new group member, or colleague knows the

damnable anxiousness of having to guess, imagine, or figure out ways of asking what the answer is. Not knowing the answer(s) to this basic question is much more difficult to deal with than knowing the answer(s), no matter what the final judgment, and it is more disruptive to the possibilities of cooperative or collaborative work.

There is a personal element in every task that people do together, whether it be teaching and learning, designing circuitry, or discussing metaphysics. How persons think and feel about each other and about what they are doing holds great powers for inhibition or release of talent, effort, and cooperative achievement. Able persons can be effectively disabled by uncertainty about their relation to the people around them. Such uncertainty is a part of the fear of expressing deeply felt opinions, of trying to do difficult or previously untried things (some people would call that being creative), and even in some cases, of doing anything that others will see and judge. So-called underachievement and the so-called reading problem of dyslexia are examples of this uncertainty; they are symptoms of fear, fear of others because we don't know what they think of us, and because that question is so much more important than any other. (See Laing, 1967 and 1969, and Goffman, 1963, for a fuller treatment of the effects of fear.)

The question of what others think and feel about us is benign enough when we think others are ignorant of us and therefore would have little to say, but it turns malignant when we suspect that others really could respond but they don't or won't. The problems this question raises concern me here only in the context of learning and working cooperatively, not in the more therapeutic context of personal analysis or the highly abstracted context of "total communication." To the extent that uncertainties provoke unnecessary misunderstandings which get in the way of learning and working together, they can and should be dealt with. Each of us has sufficient "disabilities" without an added burden of this most ridiculous kind.

two methods of misunderstanding

Certain misunderstandings are inevitable, but they needn't be permanent. They happen because we don't check every point of communication all the time to make sure that it is received clearly, without distortion. We all have some faith, some assumptions, and some habits that stimulate our interest and keep us from getting bogged down in one conversation for the rest of our lives. If we don't stop to check out these heuristics now and then, however, we run the risk of perpetuating a mistaken perception into a point of view or theory which may limit further perception and end in dogmatic disclaimers of the validity of *others'* perceptions.

Another kind of misunderstanding was made clear to me by Joseph Luft (1969, pp. 143-4) in his very important statement that

A form of cruelty in human interaction is to deliberately misunderstand the other. It is not simply misunderstanding however; rather it is misunderstanding based on understanding. A good fight or argument is one in which you come away feeling you've exchanged differences, but that the other person understands what you feel and mean. A nasty fight is one in which the other deliberately misconstrues what you think. He acts in a manner that says you are not coming through at all the way you think you are.

This sort of thing demonstrates a malicious use of the knowledge that people are concerned about what others think and feel about them, for not only does it intentionally further unconnectedness, it produces more feelings of uncertainty. It is a ploy used to avoid facing an issue brought up by another person, and to simulate control of that person. One example of this ploy is the person who pays more attention to the other's vocabulary than to his intention, who criticizes the use of words so that the point becomes lost, the communicative intention frustrated. "A little misunderstanding," constructed this way, is effective in keeping people at bay.

The simple point of this is that if we could manage to share with each other just a little more of our thoughts and feelings about each other and about the work we are trying to do together, we would be more comfortable, less impeded by unnecessary confusion, and more able to do good work and enjoy it. Children on their own manage to do this quite well, and we were all children once. Further, children do not worry about "baring their souls" to each other; they are simply upfront about things that are important to whatever they are doing.

static understanding

Understanding is an achievement. If it involves another person, it is a *joint* achievement. (Few things are so irritating as being told by someone that he understands you, when you know damn well that you haven't given him a clue and his "understanding" is based on some theory or other.) Frequently a teacher falls into the trap of trying to understand a student by talking him over with other teachers or with the counsellor, or by giving him a number of tests. Both procedures avoid direct contact with the student, and thus prevent any possibility that "understanding" will be a shared venture. The procedures show greater respect for methods than for persons, and a crippling split between "ideas" and experience. When his ideas become fixed into rigid general methods of dealing with people, a teacher runs the risk of becoming blind to the actual experiences he undergoes. Only such blindness could cause a teacher to use the same materials, plans, and methods year after year, for to him all classes must look the same — or they will look the same by the end of the year.

Each class is, as Luft puts it, unique as a fingerprint. When this is lost sight of, teaching becomes a bore, the teacher a functionary of closed experience, the grading curve predictable, and June jejune.

> To be open to experience means . . . that we cannot repeat past successes with past techniques. We cannot organize the educational event in advance. . . . there is a point beyond which our tendency to organize becomes inimical to experience, inimical to teaching.

This point of Dennison's (1969, p. 258) is basic to the problem of remaining a teacher for more than one year. Organized repetition is the enemy of growth and therefore of important learning. A teacher is not supposed to be an enemy of learning in others or in himself. I would go on to agree with Dennison (p. 260) that ". . . we cannot speak of teaching and learning at all unless we speak of ways and means of sustaining the powers that are visible in the child when first he comes to class." If a teacher works out of a method, his expectations precede each student and the expectations act to restrict the student's visibility to within the parameters of the method. When this happens, the student's powers are lost unless he is lucky enough to fall naturally within the method, and with loss of powers go the footing of self-respect and the very roots of motivation. While the method is served, the students wait. And wait. And they get static, in both senses.

heeding and teaching

"Heed" comes from the Anglo-Saxon *hedan*, which had the sense of keeping care, protection. I think heeding is more of a disposition than a discrete behavior, more of an attitude one has in doing things than any particular thing done. I also think that it is an essential disposition for being a good teacher; care-full attention draws persons near each other in care-filling ways. Helping people to deal better with what they care about and helping them to take care of themselves is the point of teaching. (I think that's what the term *relevance* is supposed to mean.)

An experience I had during this writing (an eight-hour talk with a close friend) taught me something that has a lot to do with teaching in a heedful way. Our talk was about a twist that had happened in our friendship. I had noticed that my friend had stopped coming to visit me as often as he had in the past, and that when I went to his house we were less happy even though we still talked a lot. We weren't taking care of our friendship very well, and we wanted to find out why. So we talked about it. I learned that whenever we got together I would turn the conversation to some heavy, serious, work-problem pressures. I would turn our conversations themselves into work, into problems without end. There is nothing wrong in that, he told me (and I agreed), but it was happening *all the time*. As soon as he saw me coming, he could predict what was going to happen, and the very predictability made our time together increasingly depressing and tedious. We had been friends for almost ten years, learning immensely from each other and with each other, and yet those few months became very bad for both of us. The difference was that I had become so intense about solving problems, about *not wasting time* when there was so much to do, that we couldn't relax together. The result was that we wasted all our time together. I was trying so hard not to waste time and he was so busy indulging me that we very blindly stopped sharing anything at all. After our talk we had learned another part of taking care of each other, of our friendship, and we both knew that we could go on learning from and with each other.

After thinking about this experience for a long time, it began to occur to me that if a teacher feels a pressure not to "waste time," to make everything that happens in class a "lesson" (in the old scheme of things) or a "problematic situation" (in the new scheme of the same things), in short, if the kids can predict what's going to happen when they meet the teacher, the class may be heading for depression and tedium. Too much uninterrupted learning of one kind is a drag, just as too much uninterrupted anything is a drag. A conscientious, efficient, deliberate, consistent, serious, ever-informa-tive teacher runs the risk of teaching, inadvertently, that his classes are to be avoided. Everybody eventually gets tired of walking into wholly predictable situations. Setting up such situations is not very heedful or care-full of the persons for whom the situations are presumably designed. Being overly concerned about making time count might lead to an absolute waste of time because stopping to consider people's cares will be seen as *interruptions*, unnecessary to the task at hand. As these interruptions are systematically screened out of a situa-tion, the situation becomes careless in terms of people. It is not difficult to imagine how a person feels about those who treat him carelessly.

What I am suggesting here is contrary to a rather tradi-tional notion that if a teacher tries to become friends with his students, they will lose respect for him or he will lose control of the class or he will be creating difficulties for himself in terms of maintaining discipline. I've always had trouble un-derstanding that notion because I've thought all along that friendship is based on respect, and that people who respect each other don't have to resort to disciplining each other. From one point of view it is easier to teach without being friends, as Jonathan Kozol has said (1967, p. 115): "Keeping a teacher from being a friend to a child (enables) the teacher to deny for his own comfort the complicated nature of every person of any kind who is alive." From another point of view it is intolerable not to be friends with the students if one ex-pects to teach (p. 158): "The real reason that I was able to get on with those children in the state in which I found them is that I came into that room knowing myself to be absolutely on their side." People who are friends are on each other's side;

people who are not friends are on "the other side." People who are on the same side cooperate with each other; people who are on "the other side" work against each other or ignore each other. It makes sense to heed friendship itself if one wishes to become involved in teaching and learning with others, which is another way of saying to become involved in care-filled cooperation. Sylvia Ashton-Warner, one of the best heeders I know of, sums up her experience this way (1967, p. 53):

> From the teacher's end it boils down to whether or not she is a good conversationalist; whether or not she has the gift or the wisdom to listen to another; the ability to draw out and preserve that other's line of thought.

It's hard to explain why so few people in American schools recognize the tremendous effects of good conversation on thinking and learning and friendship. It's also hard to see why so few adults even believe that it's possible to have a good conversation with a child—let alone with each other. Most of those who teach about teaching assume that it's not possible. They constantly worry themselves over making up new techniques and inventing various gimmicks and gimcrackery to take the place of the main functions of conversation, namely, sharing information, experiencing personal involvement, and pursuing something that one wants to know more about until one knows more about it.

I am not arguing against all techniques and systems for handling information. I would simply like to see them used as adjuncts or supplements to the more basic, heedful, cooperative, conversant relations that need to exist between teachers and students before either can help the other foster his learning, growth, and happiness, and before any system will make sense.

To help another in this way, you have to know what the other needs, and the only way to find out what the other needs is for him to tell you. And he won't tell you unless he thinks you will listen to him carefully. And the way to convince him that you will listen to him carefully is to listen to him carefully. It is very difficult to talk with a system, because systems only hear what they want to hear, which is very sloppy listening indeed. A person who is performing a technique on students and making judgments in terms of the technique is behaving like a system.

A teacher who would try to help others learn through heedful conversation instead of through the execution of a technique or a system will find that a syllabus is of little value. He probably will find also that "All authorities get nervous when learning is conducted without a syllabus" (Postman and Weingartner, 1969, p. 30). A nervous authority tends to fire people who make it nervous, so beware. Yes, beware of good conversations because you might get fired for being part of them on the school grounds.

references

Archambault, R. D. 1965. *Philosophical analysis and education.* London: Routledge and Kegan Paul.

Ashton-Warner, Sylvia. 1967. *Teacher.* New York: Bantam.

Becker, Ernest. 1968. *The structure of evil.* New York: Braziller.

————. 1969. *Angel in armor.* New York: Braziller.

Bellow, Saul. 1969. *Mr. Sammler's planet.* New York: Viking.

Bertalanffy, Ludwig von. 1967. *Robots, men and minds.* New York: Braziller.

Birnbaum, Max. 1969. Sense and non-sense about sensitivity training. *Saturday Review,* Nov. 15.

Bohm, David. 1958. *Quantum theory.* Englewood Cliffs, N.J.: Prentice-Hall.

Bradford, L. P.; Gibb, J. R.; and Benne, K. D., eds. 1964. *T-group theory and laboratory method.* New York: Wiley.

Bronowski, J. 1965. *Science and human values.* New York: Harper Torchbooks.

Bruner, Jerome S. 1964. *On knowing.* Cambridge: Belknap Press.

Buchanan, Scott. 1929. *Poetry and mathematics.* New York: Lippincott. (Reissued 1962.)

Bugenthal, James F. T. 1965. *The search for authenticity.* New York: Holt, Rinehart and Winston.

————, ed. 1967. *Challenges of humanistic psychology.* New York: McGraw-Hill.

Burgess, Anthony. 1968. The future of Anglo-American. *Harper's,* Feb.

Burrow, Trigant. 1927. *The social basis of consciousness.* London: Kegan Paul.

Burton, Arthur, ed. 1969. *Encounter.* San Francisco: Jossey-Bass.

Camus, Albert. 1946. *The stranger.* New York: Vintage.

————. 1955. *The myth of Sisyphus.* New York: Vintage.

Cartwright, Dorwin, and Zander, Alvin, eds. 1967. *Group dynamics.* 3rd ed. New York: Harper and Row.

Chenault, J. 1966. Syntony: a philosophical premise for theory and research. *Journal of Humanistic Psychology* 6:31–36.

Clark, Donald H. 1969. *Permission to grow: education and the exploration of human potential.* New York: Carnegie Corporation.

Cleaver, Eldridge. 1968. *Soul on ice.* New York: McGraw-Hill.

De Lay, Donald H., and Nyberg, David. 1970. If your school stinks, CRAM it. *Phi Delta Kappan* 51:310–12.

Demos, R. 1939. *The philosophy of Plato.* New York: Scribner's.

Dennison, George. 1969. *The lives of children.* New York: Random House.

Dewey, John. 1934. *A common faith.* New Haven, Conn.: Yale University Press.

———. 1958. *Experience and nature.* New York: Dover.

———. 1960a. *Experience, nature and freedom,* ed. R. J. Bernstein. New York: Bobbs-Merrill.

———. 1960b. *Quest for certainty.* New York: Capricorn.

———. 1961. *Democracy and education.* New York: Macmillan.

———. 1967. *Lectures in the philosophy of education,* ed. R. D. Archambault. New York: Random House.

Farson, Richard E. 1969. How can anything that feels so bad be so good? *Saturday Review,* Sept. 6.

Friedenberg, Edgar Z. 1965. *The dignity of youth and other atavisms.* Boston: Beacon.

Friedlander, Paul. 1958. *Plato,* vol. 1. New York: Pantheon.

———. 1964. *Plato,* vol. 2. New York: Pantheon.

Galt, William. 1933. *Phyloanalysis.* London: Kegan Paul.

Goffman, Erving. 1963. *Stigma.* Englewood Cliffs, N.J.: Prentice-Hall.

Goodman, Paul. 1956. *Growing up absurd.* New York: Vintage.

Heisenberg, W. 1952. *Philosophic problems of nuclear science.* New York: Pantheon.

Henry, Jules. 1963. *Culture against man.* New York: Random House.

———. 1966a. Sham. Paper prepared for the Conference on Society and Psychosis, the Hahnemann Medical College, October.

———. 1966b. Vulnerability in education. *Teachers College Record* 68:135–45.

Herndon, James. 1965. *The way it spozed to be.* New York: Simon and Schuster.

Hilgard, Ernest. 1966. The human dimension in teaching. *Delta News-Journal*, Stanford University, winter, pp. 3–13.

Holt, John. 1964. *How children fail.* New York: Dell.

————. 1967. *How children learn.* New York: Pitman.

————. 1969. *The underachieving school.* New York: Pitman.

Jaspers, Karl. 1962. *The great philosophers.* New York: Harcourt, Brace and World.

Jourard, Sidney M. 1958. *Personal adjustment: an approach through the study of healthy personality.* New York: Macmillan.

————. 1964. *The transparent self.* Princeton, N.J.: Van Nostrand.

————. 1968. *Disclosing man to himself.* Princeton, N.J.: Van Nostrand.

Kaplan, Abraham. 1964. *The conduct of inquiry.* San Francisco: Chandler.

Koestler, Arthur. 1964. *The act of creation.* New York: Macmillan.

Kohl, Herbert. 1967a. *Teaching the "unteachable."* New York: New York Review.

————. 1967b. *36 children.* New York: New American Library.

————. 1969. *The open classroom.* New York: Vintage.

Kozol, Jonathan. 1967. *Death at an early age.* Boston: Houghton Mifflin.

Kuhn, Thomas S. 1964. *The structure of scientific revolutions.* Chicago: Phoenix Books.

Laing, R. D. 1967. *The politics of experience.* New York: Pantheon.

————. 1969. *The self and others.* New York: Pantheon.

Leonard, George B. 1968. *Education and ecstasy.* New York: Delacorte.

Luft, Joseph. 1969. *Of human interaction.* Palo Alto, Calif.: National Press Books.

————. 1970. *Group processes.* 2nd ed. Palo Alto, Calif.: National Press Books.

Marin, Peter. 1969. The open truth and fiery vehemence of youth: a sort of soliloquy. *The Center Magazine*, vol. 2, no. 1, pp. 61–74.

McGlashan, Alan. 1967. *The savage and beautiful country.* Boston: Houghton Mifflin.

Moustakas, Clark. 1961. *Loneliness*. Englewood Cliffs, N.J.: Prentice-Hall.

——. 1966. *The authentic teacher*. Cambridge, Mass.: Doyle.

Nyberg, David. 1970. In between in and out: overcoming nondirective leadership. *Human Relations Training News*, vol. 14, no. 3, pp. 1–3.

Perls, Frederick; Hefferline, R. F.; and Goodman, Paul. 1951. *Gestalt therapy*. New York: Delta.

Planck, Max. 1936. *The philosophy of physics*. New York: Norton.

Plato. 1961. *The collected dialogues*, eds. E. Hamilton and H. Cairns. New York: Pantheon.

Polanyi, Michael. 1958. *Personal knowledge*. Chicago: University of Chicago Press.

——. 1964. *Science, faith and society*. Chicago: Phoenix Books.

——. 1966. *The tacit dimension*. Garden City, N.Y.: Doubleday.

Postman, Neil, and Weingartner, Charles. 1969. *Teaching as a subversive activity*. New York: Delacorte.

Rogers, Carl R. 1942. *Counseling and psychotherapy*. Boston: Houghton Mifflin.

——. 1951. *Client-centered therapy*. Boston: Houghton Mifflin.

——. 1958. Characteristics of a helping relationship. *Personal Guidance Journal* 37:6–16.

——. 1961. *On becoming a person*. Boston: Houghton Mifflin.

——. 1969. *Freedom to learn*. Columbus, Ohio: Merrill.

Rosenthal, Robert, and Jacobson, Lenore. 1968. *Pygmalion in the classroom*. New York: Holt, Rinehart and Winston.

Schein, Edgar H., and Bennis, Warren G., eds. 1965. *Personal and organizational change through group methods*. New York: Wiley.

Schwab, Joseph J. 1969. *College curriculum and student protest*. Chicago: University of Chicago Press.

Seashore, C.; Kimple, J.; and Kinney, G. 1969. Sensitivity training: can it work in the schools? *Nation's Schools*, vol. 83, no. 3.

Shanner, William M. n.d. PLAN: a system of individualized instruction utilizing currently available instructional materials. Westinghouse Learning Corporation paper.

Strawson, P. F. 1963. *Individuals*. New York: Anchor.

Thomas, Lawrence G. 1968. Implications of transaction theory. *The Educational Forum*, January, pp. 145–55.

Wann, T. W., ed. 1964. *Behaviorism and phenomenology*. Chicago: University of Chicago Press.

Watts, Alan W. 1966. *The book*. New York: Collier.

──────. 1968. *The wisdom of insecurity*. New York: Vintage.

Whitehead, Alfred North. 1967. *Science and the modern world*. New York: The Free Press.

──────. 1968. *Modes of thought*. New York: The Free Press.

Wilson, Colin. 1967. *Introduction to the new existentialism*. Boston: Houghton Mifflin.